Project Management in Construction

PROJECT MANAGEMENT IN CONSTRUCTION

Dennis Lock

GOWER

© Dennis Lock 2004

Published by
Gower Publishing Limited
Gower House
Croft Road
Aldershot
Hants GU11 3HR
England

Gower Publishing Company
Suite 420
101 Cherry Street
Burlington
VT 05401-4405
USA

Dennis Lock has asserted his right under the Copyright, Designs and Patents Act, 1988 to be identified as the author of this work.

British Library Cataloguing in Publication Data
Lock, Dennis, 1929-
    Project management in construction
    1. Project management 2. Construction industry – Management
    I. Title
    624' .0684

    ISBN 0 566 08612 3

Library of Congress Cataloging-in-Publication Data
Lock, Dennis.
    Project management in construction / by Dennis Lock.
        p. cm.
    Includes bibliographical references and index.
    ISBN 0-566-08612-3
    1. Construction industry--Management. 2. Production management. I. Title.
    HD9715.A2L624 2004
    624'.068'4--dc22

                                                                            2004002703

Typeset by Secret Genius, 11 Mons Court, Winchester SO23 8GH
Printed in Great Britain by MPG Books Ltd, Bodmin, Cornwall

Contents

P45.

Chapter 11 – Controlling Changes

Chapter 12 – Handover and Close-out

List of Figures

List of Tables

Innovations in production and project management over the last 100 years were driven first by the manufacturing companies and, later, by the aerospace and defence industries. The construction industry has a long record of project management practice and is well recognized for using or adapting appropriate project management methods and software to good effect. Even in the early 1970s I knew of construction companies that were planning their projects in novel and imaginative ways that today might still be considered advanced. It's always good to be writing for an appreciative audience, so when I was invited to work on this book in collaboration with the Construction Industry Training Board I jumped at the chance. I have not been disappointed, and this has proved to be one of my most enjoyable writing engagements.

Project management spans many management disciplines and relies on a wide range of diverse technical and managerial skills. The average construction project manager must be able to communicate and work with the client, the company accountant, the bank, the purchasing manager, the architect, the design engineer, specialists and contractors in specialist trades, site supervisors, the human resources manager, lawyers, insurers, various professional bodies, and with local authority officers and other statutory bodies. The construction industry, like many others, is awash with regulations, some of which carry severe penalties if they are flouted. So project management can be a very broad subject, impossible to cover fully in a single introductory textbook.

However, if we pare away all the ancillary topics, a small group of essential core project management skills remains. These are the methods by which a project is organized, planned and controlled. These are the essential processes needed to ensure that the project meets the three primary objectives of cost, time and performance or, in other words, that the project is finished to the mutual satisfaction of the client and the contractor. But confining the discussion to these core elements still leaves a wide range of possible topics because the project management methods chosen will depend to a large extent on the size and nature of the project. Even the objectives themselves are not always clear-cut, and there will always be other 'stakeholders', apart from the client and the contractor, whose wishes must be taken into account.

So, writing about project management could be seen as a daunting task. What should I have included and what should have been left out? However, my work was made considerably easier by the knowledge that this book has companion volumes that deal specifically with other important related topics. That left me free to concentrate on the core issues, so that is what I have done.

A few large projects need very sophisticated techniques but most projects are relatively small and can be managed with a mix of common sense and fairly straightforward methods. Every successful modern construction company of significant size has at least one project support office or planning group. Thus the large construction groups are not short of experts when it comes to dealing with very large projects. So this book is intended as an introduction for those who are new to the subject, starting with projects at the smaller end of the scale.

I start by describing topics that are best suited to very small projects. Later chapters are organized to some extent so that they gradually become more relevant to larger and more complex projects. So the reader who has a small family business will probably need to read only the first few chapters. But, as that family business expands and the projects (and, we hope, the profits) become larger, he or she can revisit this book and delve into the later chapters. There is a short list of titles at the end for those who would like to read further into the subject of this rewarding profession.

I cannot end this Preface without acknowledging the support that I have received from senior members of the Construction Industry Training Board. I must also thank Robert Pow, whose wide experience of the insurance industry was invaluable for Chapter 8. Finally, I am indebted to Dr David J. Cooper of the University of Salford, consulting editor for this series, for his advice and constructive criticism, both of an early draft and of the final manuscript.

Dennis Lock
St Albans
2004

This book starts with chapters for those new to project management – people who are carrying out simple construction projects in small (perhaps family-run) businesses. Some of the later chapters will be of more interest to those who already have some experience of project management and explain methods that are more applicable to larger companies and more complex projects. Thus some readers will not need to read all the chapters, at least on their first visit to this book. Here, therefore, is a suggested initial reading plan.

For all readers, irrespective of company size:

Chapters 1, 2, 3, 9, 10, 11 and the last section of Chapter 12.

For readers working in medium- to large-sized companies, especially those handling larger projects:

Chapters 4, 5, 6, 7, 8 and all of Chapter 12.

We all need skills. Just look around.

**Take a look around any construction site in the UK and you'll find
highly skilled people; many individuals from the 35,000 people per
annum, both Adults and New Entrants (apprentices) who we have
trained to enhance not only their careers, but also the companies
they work for.**

Look closer at any one of our four superb college sites across the UK, in
Birmingham, Glasgow, Erith or Bircham Newton in Norfolk and you'll see
the best instructors and the best facilities. We can even offer this same
excellent standard of training at your own premises or a local training
venue.

As the UK's leading construction skills training suppliers, we offer not
only the best training, we also give you free professional advice on
finding the right training, assistance in sourcing grant aid, building
customized training courses and ultimately delivering the skills that you'll
need.

If you're looking for, quite simply, the best construction skills training,
look no further than the National Construction College and you'll see a
way to a great future in the Construction Industry.

**For high quality yet cost effective
training, call us now on:
08475 336666
for Adult training
01485 577669
for Apprentice training**

Investors in People, ISO 9001:2000 and City and Guilds accredited.

 National Construction College

Chapter 1

Introducing Project Management

You are a master builder and you are good at your job. You know a brick from a breeze block. Give you a new site, put plans in your hands, and you will know how to build that extension, put up a new house – or even two houses. Clear the site. Put up a fence to keep out kids, vandals and thieves. Measure and mark out. Don't hold the plans upside down. Hire the plant. Dig the footings, and start building. You've done it all before. You expect to do it again somewhere else. You would never do anything silly, like starting on the electrics before the roof is on. You know when to call in your special trades. You get all the materials on site at the right time. You cope with bad weather. You might not realize it, but you are managing a project. It's all just plain logic and common sense, and you don't need some smartarse in pinstripes to tell you how to do it.

Project management: simply common sense.

A project means doing something new, possibly even something risky or adventurous. In the business world this usually means creating something that someone else wants and is prepared to pay for. Most projects have targets, which means they have to be built right, within a cost budget, and finished by a certain date. Project management is simply making sure that all these targets are met.

Common-sense principles of project management

However big or small your project, there are a few things that must be done if you are to get it right. These are listed below, and some are explained more fully in later chapters.

1 Know your project. Define it. Find out exactly what you have to do. Which jobs will you be paid for and which jobs are someone else's responsibility? Are there any special conditions? Checklists are useful to make sure that you don't forget anything at this stage.

Two key project factors:
1   Logic
2   Checklists

2 Estimate the costs as accurately as you can. Construction managers are fortunate in this respect because they can use standard tables, such as those in the price books published by Spon (http://www.sponpress.com).

3 Make sure that your estimates allow for contingencies, provisional items and (for projects lasting several years) for cost escalation. These are often called the below-the-line costs (explained in Chapter 2).

4 Know your customer or customers. Can they afford to pay you? Have they given others trouble in the past? You might need to make some discreet enquiries. For company investigations, agencies such as Dunn and Bradstreet can be useful (http://www.dnb.com).

5 Is the contract understood and agreed by all parties? In construction, standard forms are often used, which help to remove possible misunderstandings and save time in lawyers' fees. There are standard forms for main contracts and for some special subcontracts (installing lifts, for example).

6 Will your cash flow be up to the job? You might have to pay workers and suppliers before the customer's cheque reaches your bank. Your contract should allow for an initial deposit and stage payments from the customer to help cover your work-in-progress costs. Stay on friendly terms with your bank!

7 Have a plan. The method used will depend on the size and scope of the project. For a tiny project it might be in your head. But most projects need something a little more sophisticated, put down on paper. The last 50 years have seen big advances in planning methods.

8 Know how to measure work done against your plan and be prepared to take action as soon as you notice things starting to go wrong. Work measurement, certified by a quantity surveyor, is important if you are going to make stage claims for payment from your customer.

9 Control changes. Make sure that every change requested by the customer is covered by a contract variation order with adequate price cover.

10 Take steps to keep inconvenience to the public at a minimum. You might need to take special steps to keep the public informed to avoid adverse reactions or even disruptive interference.

11 Pay regard to health and safety. Know and obey the regulations, have a health and safety policy and carry sufficient insurance.

12 Think about site security. Nothing is safe from thieves, from the smallest hand-tools to bulk materials and the biggest hire plant. Fence the site to keep valuables in and vandals out.

13 Don't be afraid to get professional help from the architect, surveyor, lawyer, accountant, tax expert and so on, so that potential problems get nipped in the bud. You might save yourself from tripping over some of the red tape that seems to be everywhere these days.

Project success or failure

Project management aims to plan, organize and control a project so that it can be called a success. But how are we to tell what is meant by success?

Three primary objectives

The simplest way of defining a project as successful is to show that three primary objectives have been met. These might possibly be called the three graces of project management and they are:

- delivery or completion on or before the date agreed with the customer
- completion within the budgeted cost
- a building that meets the set standards of quality.

Three critical objectives:
1   Time
2   Cost
3   Specification

Budget

All work should be carried out against budgets. For a small builder this is just a list of jobs annotated with their estimated labour and material costs. For larger projects built by some of the bigger contracting companies, budgets will exist not only for jobs, but also for each of the head office departments involved and for other elements of the project and its organization.

When actual costs exceed their budgets the contractor's profits are at risk. If the losses are very great, the contractor's business is at risk. The project might even have to be aborted, or restarted with a fresh contractor.

A project that costs more than intended might not be a failure. If the contractor can complete the overspent project successfully and stay in business, and if the contract was agreed at a fixed price, then the project purchaser at least should be satisfied. The contractor should, of course, learn from his mistake. Some cost control measures are given in Chapter 7.

Delivery or handover on time

Time is often the most important objective of all. Time is an irreplaceable resource. A job that has missed its target date is late and that, unfortunately, is that. Costs tend to follow time and grow with time. A project that is finished late usually also overruns its budgets. So, controlling progress against the plan goes a long way towards controlling the costs of a project. Chapter 8 deals with some ways of controlling progress.

Time is money: Benjamin Franklin (1748) in Advice to a Young Tradesman

Quality

The project should meet all specifications in respect of appearance, safety, reliability and performance.

Balancing the three primary objectives

The three primary objectives are all interrelated. For example, time is usually related to costs. Project owners sometimes have to decide whether or not more emphasis should be given to one of the objectives, perhaps at the expense of the other two.

A special word is needed in this context about quality. Many writers (including myself when young) have listed 'quality' as one of the three primary objectives of project management. A good, generally accepted definition of quality is that the object should be fit for its intended purpose. Of course *every* project must be fit for its intended purpose. So, 'quality' as such is an objective that is not negotiable: it is an absolute requirement and cannot be part of an objectives balancing exercise.

Quality is not negotiable. The project must be fit for its intended purpose.

However, consider two different building schemes, each for a block of residential apartments. One is a luxury block where the developer expects to receive high rents from rich tenants. The other is a local authority project to provide basic accommodation for families with low or no means of support. One of these developments might have en-suite bathrooms with gold-plated fittings, marble floors, two garage spaces per flat, with the whole set in landscaped grounds. The local authority building will probably display concrete as one of its main features. But each of these projects is intended for a different purpose and, if fit for that purpose when finished, can be called a quality success.

So what we often mean when we write about 'quality' in the context of balancing objectives is the *level of specification*. Here are some examples where balancing decisions must be made:

1   A nuclear power station must above all be reliable and safe. So the quality objective is paramount.

2   A project to build a stadium for the Olympic Games must be ready in time for the games. So time is the paramount objective.

3   A hospital management group needs to build an extension to act as consulting rooms and waiting areas for outpatients. The budgets are very limited. So the specification must be trimmed so that the cost is as low as possible.

4   A charitable institution, strapped for cash, is housed in a building that has been condemned. So, a project to provide a new building is urgent. Here time and budget share the top priority, with the level of specification coming third.

Wider concerns of stakeholders

The principal parties to most small- to medium-sized construction contracts will be the purchaser, or client, and the contractor. As principal stakeholders, each of these will have a strong vested interest in the success of the project. But others will also have an interest. To take a rather obvious case, look at Figure 1.1. An office building is nearing completion at a road junction, on one side of which stands a modest house. It is most unlikely that the householder will welcome this new building, which cuts light and will give the office workers direct line of vision into all the house windows. Yet others will welcome the new building. Local shopkeepers can look forward to increased trade and the office workers themselves should appreciate their move into modern, well lit and air-conditioned accommodation.

Figure 1.1 *A successful project? Not everyone would agree*

Larger projects will be discussed later in this book, particularly in respect of their planning and organization. It is convenient to take a preliminary glimpse at one of these projects now, to examine the possible reactions of all the stakeholders involved. The project is a shopping mall development in a town centre.

The principal stakeholders in this project might be listed as:

- the property developer
- the landowner
- the main contractor
- the local authority
- the bank or financing institution.

Another group of stakeholders, just one notch down from the principals just listed, would include:

- the architect
- subcontractors
- construction workers
- companies taking space in the new shops
- the company operating the car parks.

But there are many more people and organizations that might be affected in one way or another by this big town-centre development. They include, but are not limited to:

- local residents in adjacent properties
- estate agents
- shopkeepers of existing shops whose trade might be affected
- passers-by
- motorists
- potential shoppers
- the emergency services
- companies that will supply goods to the shops
- companies that will provide services to the shops
- shopworkers
- maintenance companies engaged on various service contracts, such as servicing of elevators and lifts, window cleaning and much more.

Some might disagree with the rankings in these lists but it is clear that any large project will affect stakeholders from a number of sources in different ways. Each stakeholder will have his or her different view of the way in which the three primary objectives should be balanced. Some will be against the project altogether.

The most successful project is the one that satisfies all the stakeholders. That is a very difficult objective that is not always possible to achieve but, as project managers, we should at least try.

Chapter **2**

Planning Small Projects

This chapter introduces the important subject of project planning, but is confined to simple methods that are suitable for small projects and need no special equipment or training.

Managing a very tiny project with simple logic and common sense

The case study described below was a very tiny project carried out by a plumber and his assistant.

The Boiler Project

Mrs Brown wanted a new hot water system installed in her bungalow. The old, scale-clogged system had a free-standing solid-fuel boiler in the kitchen, heating water directly in an adjacent unlagged tank which was also fitted with an electric immersion heater. With white hot coke, a glowing flue and thunderous burps and gurgles, it's a wonder that the whole lot did not take off and vanish through the roof in a shower of steam and sparks.

To fail to plan is to plan to fail.

The replacement system needed a header tank, new boiler and flue, new hot water cylinder with primary and secondary water circuits, new immersion heater and new mains wiring. Not a difficult job by any means, but there was one snag. Mrs Brown made it clear that she did not want to suffer any evening without plenty of hot water from her taps.

The contractor solved the problem using simple logic and common sense. The project was achieved in three separate stages over three days. This is how it was done:

Day 1   Drain down. Disconnect, dismantle and remove the old boiler and flue and cart them away. Cap off the old tank boiler feeds. Turn on the water and refill the old tank. Now Mrs Brown can have all the hot water she needs, using the old immersion heater. The new boiler and flue can now be assembled and fixed in place.

Day 2   Drain down. Remove the old hot water tank and immersion heater and cart them away. Install the new hot water cylinder and temporarily connect it to water pipes from the big loft tank. Now Mrs Brown can get hot tap water from the new cylinder using the electric immersion heater.

Day 3   Fit the new small header tank, and connect the primary heater pipes and expansion pipe to the new boiler. Fill up the boiler with coke, light it and test the boiler for leaks and heating. Lag the cylinder and pipework. Job done. Mrs Brown delighted.

Perhaps this plumber was gifted with slightly more than average common sense and he certainly showed a remarkable degree of respect for Mrs Brown's wishes and commanding manner. But no special project management skills were used. This case will be revisited briefly later in this chapter to demonstrate a simple planning tool that could have been used to put the plan on paper and rely less on the plumber's memory and brainpower.

When common sense is not enough

Returning to the broader world of construction management, imagine now that you decide to team up with a business partner, so that you can expand your business in a modest way. Your projects might now be a little bigger – perhaps three or four houses on one site and another three or four projects waiting or even started. You have a small number of regular helpers or employees. You know where to go for materials, and if you look like running short you have your mobile phone and can call for fresh deliveries. You have to give your specialists, such as the chippy, plumber, roofer, glazier and electrician, some idea of dates when they will be needed and you must keep in touch with the local buildings inspector. Your different projects have different clients and different architects and you are expected now to go to the occasional progress meeting. So you will have to do some planning to schedule and coordinate all the work. You may not need to learn any new techniques, but you will have to find some way of putting your plans on paper, because the work is becoming too complicated to deal with in your head alone.

Plans for small projects can be simple charts. You don't have to use a computer if you don't want to, although that would give you advantages of speed and flexibility to change. A sharp pencil, eraser, squared paper, a ruler and a calendar are all you need. But as your business expands and your projects also grow in size, the time will come when you'll need to take planning methods more seriously.

Bar charts

The American industrial engineer Henry Gantt, almost 100 years ago, devised a planning chart that is very familiar in all kinds of project planning nowadays, not least in construction projects. The charts are often called Gantt charts, but we can use the more common name 'bar chart'.

Bar charts are drawn to scale and show all the important jobs in a project set out against a calendar. The tiny boiler project described in our case study could have been planned with a bar chart, as shown in Figure 2.1. It is easy to see why bar charts are a popular form of planning.

Job	Day 1	Day 2	Day 3
Drain and disconnect			
Cap off, refill old system			
Remove old boiler and flue			
Position new boiler and flue			
Drain system			
Remove old hot water tank			
Install new hot water cylinder			
Wire in immersion heater			
Fill and test			
Fit header tank			
Pipe to boiler and cylinder			
Fill primary system			
Light and test boiler			

Figure 2.1 *A tiny plumbing project planned with a bar chart*

Workshop project

The erection of a small workshop will demonstrate how a bar chart might be used to plan a small project.

Project definition and cost estimate

The first thing to do when planning any project is to define it. Our workshop will be built of brick, with a flat corrugated steel roof on a timber frame giving sufficient fall. The roof will be hidden behind capped brick parapets. The whole will be supported on a concrete raft. The workshop will have locking double timber doors mounted in a timber frame at the front elevation, with an RSJ lintel over. A galvanized steel window frame is to be included in one of the walls, with concrete sill, timber lintel and single glazing. Drainage from the gutters and downpipes will lead underground to a soakaway, which will lie underneath a concreted hard standing area for two

A man's gotta do what a man's gotta do! But if you're the project manager, do you know what you've gotta do? Make sure your project is properly defined before you start.

cars. The project scope does not include any internal fittings except the installation of four twin fluorescent lights and four twin 13-amp sockets, all wired in steel conduit and protected by a steel-clad switched fusebox. The internal walls will not be plastered and the lights are to be suspended from the roof timbers.

Some people like to start their planning by listing all the jobs and then arranging them later in their timeframe. Others prefer to go straight to the chart and sketch in the jobs directly as bars. However, we really need to list the jobs first because that will help us estimate the project cost.

The task list and cost estimate for this small project is shown in Table 2.1. For simplicity, the size of the workshop and quantities of materials are not given.

Job	Time in days	Labour cost (£)	Materials cost (£)
Clear and mark out the site	1	75	0
Dig soakaway and drain trench	1	150	0
Formwork for base	1	50	40
Concrete base	1	80	150
Cure time for concrete base	5	0	0
Position door frame	1	10	100
Build walls	5	700	750
Install window frame	–	50	75
Install RSJ lintel over doors	1	100	30
Finish brickwork	2	200	30
Cut and fit roof timbers	3	400	180
Cap parapets	1	75	40
Fit roof sheets	2	220	200
Seal roof sheets	1	110	70
Fit gutters and rainwater pipes	1	100	60
Hang doors	1	80	25
Prime doors and window frame	1	80	20
Glaze windows	1	50	30
Paint doors and windows	1	200	20
Fit door furniture	1	50	35
Concrete hard standing for cars	1	70	60
Install electrics	2	250	160
Connect electric mains supply*	1	0	0
Clear away (requires skips)	1	80	120
Total estimated costs		3180	2195

*Client will arrange connection

Table 2.1 *Workshop project task list and cost estimate*

A very small company or family business might set out the cost estimate as follows:

Item	£
Labour	3180
Materials	2195
	5375
Overheads 30%	1613
	6988
Contingency 10%	700
	7688
Mark-up 50%	3844
Selling price	11532

All these figures are for illustrative purposes only and are not intended to reflect true costs.

Below-the-line cost items

In the estimate set above, the contractor has added a contingency allowance of 10 per cent to cover unforeseen eventualities. The level of the contingency allowance will be increased if there is a high perceived risk, but will be lower, or even absent, if price competition is high. This is called a below-the-line item, because it comes after the line ruled under the main cost estimate.

What's all this going to cost? Don't forget the hidden extras.

For large projects, lasting several years, price inflation on materials and expected wage increases are all likely to increase the actual costs of the project in the later years. In such cases the contractor may decide to add an escalation allowance, calculated as an annual percentage appropriate for the expected rates of cost inflation.

Very often, the contractor is aware that part of the project cannot be adequately defined and estimated because of hidden factors that will only become apparent as the work proceeds. For example, suppose that a client calls for bids for the demolition and rebuilding of an office building, and requires that the boardroom panelling and doors are re-used in the replacement building. In this case, the contractor will regard the materials as being free-issue and will not include them in the cost estimates and resulting price. However, the contractor has a strong suspicion that when the panelling is removed from the old building it will crumble to dust as a result of some rather industrious beetles. He would then cover this risk by appending a provisional sum (often called a PC sum) to the cost estimate, which would be notified to the client as an additional price that would become payable in the event that the free-issue materials could not be used.

Bar chart – first attempt

The bar chart given in Figure 2.2 is a first attempt at converting the task list into a practicable working schedule. The actual start date for this project was not known when the plan was made, so all the dates are shown as day numbers, with the start date being taken as day 1. No weekends will be worked so there are to be five working days in each week. There are no public holidays expected during the course of this project.

How long will it take to build and where do we start?

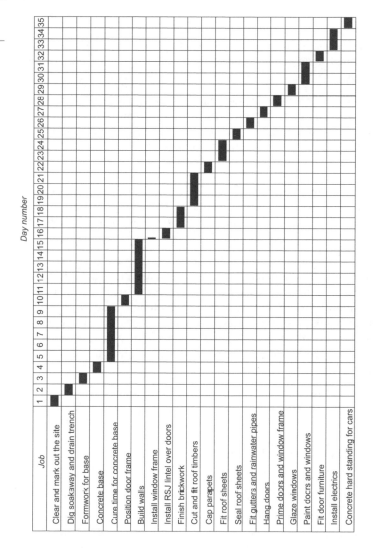

Figure 2.2 *Workshop project: an unsatisfactory bar chart*

The plan, as for all other examples in this book, has been kept as simple as possible for clarity of reproduction. For example, it does not show purchasing activities, plant hire, deliveries of materials or carting away of rubbish skips. Our cost estimate will be somewhat low as a result. The chart indicates that 35 working days will be needed. The final clear-away task is not shown, so the total duration is 36 days – just one day over seven weeks.

As the figure title suggests, the bar chart in Figure 2.2 leaves much to be desired in several respects.

Most project plans can be estimated with days as the unit of time, but in this case the unit is too coarse and half-days would have been better. For example, it will not take a whole day to make and position the formwork for the concrete base. Half-days are often convenient units for small projects, especially where there are five working days in a week, because a week is then ten units.

Another fault with the bar chart in Figure 2.2 is that it does not show weekend days. Although most jobs will not have any activity during Saturdays and Sundays, on this project paint will continue to dry over a weekend and concrete will continue to cure. So the chart should include Saturdays and Sundays for those reasons. When the chart is drawn by hand, the contractor can use his or her mental powers to determine which activities will run through weekends. When, as in later chapters of this book, a computer is used, special steps must be taken to instruct the computer as to which activities run five days per week and which can take six or seven days.

There is a fundamental flaw of logic in this first bar chart attempt. All jobs are shown in a simple sequential series. Broadly, the jobs do follow the sequence that construction would need on site but some of these jobs could take place simultaneously (provided enough workers are on hand). To take just one example, the concrete for the car hard standing area could be poured at the same time as the workshop base – provided we have not forgotten to dig the soakaway first.

So, bar charts are excellent for displaying working schedules but they are by no means the best way of working out and showing the logic of how the start of one job is dependent on the finish of another. For very small projects this can be overcome to some extent by the use of linked bar charts.

Six days thou shalt labour and do all thy work. But the seventh day is the sabbath of the LORD thy God: in it thou shalt not do any work, thou, nor thy son, nor thy daughter, nor thy man-servant, nor thy maid-servant, nor thine ox, nor thine ass, nor any of thy cattle, nor thy stranger that is within thy gates; that thy man-servant and thy maid-servant may rest as well as thou. (Deuteronomy 5: verses 13 and 14). But Microsoft Project's default calendar is five working days.

Putting the cart before the horse is never wise but can be expensive with fresh mixed concrete.

Linked bar charts

It is possible to place lines on a bar chart to show the link between the end of one job and the starts of all jobs that are then enabled to start. This simply cannot be done on large projects because the charts become too cluttered, but for this little workshop project there is no problem.

Figure 2.3 is the improved bar chart for the workshop project. Weekend days are now shown, and one or two tasks have been reduced from one day to half-day duration. Most important, more thought has been given to the logic of the plan, and it can be seen that several jobs are now scheduled to take place simultaneously.

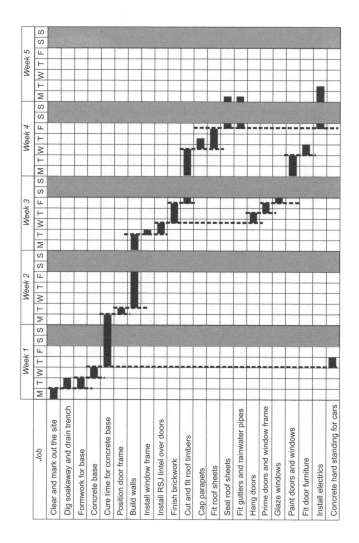

Figure 2.3 Workshop project: a bar chart with improved planning logic and inter-task links

Although the start date for this project is not yet known, we have started our plan from a Monday. By using a more logical approach and overlapping jobs where possible, the overall planned duration has been reduced from the seven weeks' duration indicated in Figure 2.2 to just over four weeks.

Bar charts for resource scheduling

When several different jobs are run together at the same time, you cannot be sure whether or not there will be enough people with the necessary skills on site. Also, it is desirable to plan the work so that the number of people needed does not change greatly from day to day. A smooth pattern of resource usage avoids peaks and troughs of activity, when on one day there are too few people to do the work but on the next people are left standing about with nothing to do. The process of achieving level resource usage is usually called resource scheduling.

Before the advent of computers and project management software (which really means before the late 1960s) all resource scheduling was done using charts. These were either drawn on squared paper, or assembled from kits using wall-mounted adjustable charts. All of these charts used the bar chart principle, and bar charts can still be used for this purpose today, provided that the project is really tiny and the scheduling problem is reasonably trivial.

The best of the charting methods used wall-mounted charts punched with holes on a 6mm grid. Plastic bars could be stuck into the holes as horizontal strips to represent jobs. The bars could be cut to scale length with a craft knife and they could be colour-coded to indicate people of different skills. Suppose that red was chosen to denote electricians, so that every job needing one electrician was represented by a red bar. Then, by scanning down each daily column the planner or project manager could see how many electricians would be needed each day to carry out the plan. Any severe irregularities in the planned workload could be overcome by delaying one or two jobs to start after the overload days, and the adjustable features of the chart made this relatively easy to do. One simply unplugged the strip of plastic from its holes and repositioned it in the new place. This simple method was fine for very small projects, but the charts took ages to set up and you can imagine the planner's despair and colourful language when the plan had to be changed for any reason.

Now there are many computer packages available that can carry out resource scheduling quickly, and are flexible to changes, although these packages are very rarely able to match the perfect smoothing that the human brain could often achieve when planning small projects with adjustable bar charts. Resource scheduling will be described at greater length in Chapter 3.

Bar chart pros and cons

Bar charts are difficult to set up for large projects, cannot show more than about 50 rows of jobs or long periods without becoming cluttered, and are very inflexible to change unless a computer is hovering in the background. Ordinary bar charts cannot show how the start of one job depends on the finish of another. Even linked bar charts, which do claim to show these relationships, have very limited scope. Yet bar charts remain very popular. There are several, quite understandable reasons why many managers, even those skilled in the computer arts, still prefer to see their project plans set out as bar charts.

Bar charts, unless the planner has tried to include too much information, offer a good visual display of all the jobs that have to be done, and the timescale allows everyone to see almost at a glance how the workload will be distributed across the days and weeks to come. No other planning system does this quite so well.

It must not be forgotten that the principal reason for doing any planning at all is to provide a basis for measuring progress and controlling the work as the project proceeds. If there is a bar chart, it will have a calendar scale along the top edge. For a live project, that calendar scale will include today's date. So, when assessing progress, the project manager first needs to find out what has been done, and then compare the result with the bar chart. Quite simply, everything to the left of today's date should be finished and everything falling in the chart column under today's date should either be in progress or just starting.

In later chapters some more sophisticated planning and scheduling methods will be described. However, even the most sophisticated project management computer programs, at the high end of the price range, have the ability to convert the plans and resource schedules calculated from many thousands of data items back into bar charts for the time schedules and into histograms for the resource usage patterns. Histograms, for those new to this subject, are simply bar charts turned on their ends, so that the bars point skywards.

What makes an effective schedule?

A seven-point checklist for a perfect schedule.

To end this chapter on planning and scheduling, here is a checklist of the factors that any project schedule should possess if it is to be effective as a management tool:

1 The plan should be made in sufficient detail to allow frequent progress checks.
2 The plan should be visually effective: its meaning should immediately be clear, even to those with no special training.

3 Tasks should be set out in their logical sequence.
4 Interdependencies between tasks should be apparent.
5 Tasks with highest priority should be highlighted in some way.
6 The plan should be achievable with the resources available, or which can be made available.
7 The plan must be flexible, so that it can be changed quickly if the project scope or objectives are changed.

Bar charts go some way towards meeting all these factors but they have their deficiencies for all projects except the very tiniest. So the following chapters will examine other planning methods that seek to satisfy all the factors in this checklist.

Chapter **3**

Planning Small Projects with Critical Path Networks

Management methods underwent considerable change around 1900, when researchers, particularly in the US, began to look more closely at management methods and styles. People like Frederick Winslow Taylor studied the way in which people worked and were managed. All of this had to do with trying to improve productivity, especially in the manufacturing industries. Henry Gantt was part of this movement and his introduction of the Gantt chart (bar chart) in the early 1900s set the scene for planning and scheduling all kinds of jobs, both in factories and for construction projects. Bar charts, usually set up on wallboards or drawn on large sheets of paper, reigned supreme for about 50 years as everybody's favourite planning method. No manager's office was complete without a bar chart on at least one wall. But bar charts do have their limitations, some of which were mentioned in the previous chapter. So people tried to find new and better planning methods, especially for projects.

If you have the time, search for <Frederick Winslow Taylor> or the <Hawthorne Experiment> on the Internet to learn about some of the giants of scientific management who flourished at the beginning of the last century.

Critical path network methods were developed independently in Britain, Belgium and the US around 1950. Because the developers worked independently, several different methods emerged and some of those early methods have fallen by the wayside. Today, one method, known as the precedence system, has become universally popular. By no means the least reason for this popularity is that today's computer programs can only work with the precedence system, and programs that could once process other network analysis methods are no longer supplied or supported. This chapter, therefore, will describe the precedence system.

Critical path network analysis: a sea change in project planning methods.

Critical path network analysis using the precedence system

Remember that bar charts are limited in the way they can display interdependencies between different jobs in a project. Linked bar charts are fine when there are only a few jobs to schedule but larger projects have hundreds – even thousands – of different tasks. So the first thing we need is a system that will let us show these interdependencies clearly on paper or on a computer screen. The precedence system does that very well.

Logical sequence of tasks

Figure 3.1 shows how the preferred and logical sequence of project jobs can be shown in a precedence diagram. Each box in the diagram represents a project job, which is always called an *activity* or a *task* (it doesn't matter which) in the jargon of critical path networks. The action in any network diagram always flows from left to right, so the arrowheads are not really necessary and are often not used. So the chart in Figure 3.1 clearly depicts six tasks needed to complete a tiny project, with the tasks laid out in their logical and most practical sequence. Of course all projects have more than six tasks, but it is easier to explain how precedence diagrams are used if at first we keep everything very simple. So we shall refer to this in the following paragraphs as Project Simple. We can move on to projects of a more realistic size later.

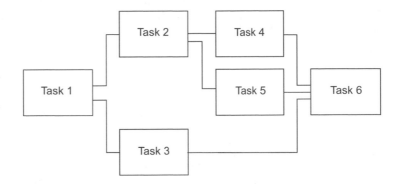

All critical path networks drive from left to right.

Figure 3.1 *Logical sequence of tasks in a precedence network diagram*

A network should have only one start and one finish task.

We usually prefer to have only one start task and one finish task in a network, as seen in Figure 3.1. When a network does have more than one start or finish task it is convenient to invent artificial start and finish tasks for this purpose. Task 1 might then be 'Project start' and task 6 in our example could be 'Project finish and handover'.

The logic will be clear to anyone used to working with engineering flowcharts, but in any case is easy to follow. It is understood that task 2 cannot start until task 1 has been finished. Likewise, task 6 cannot start before tasks 3, 4 and 5 have all been finished.

In practice the task names or descriptions would be written inside the boxes too. The task numbers (ID codes) are especially important if the plan is going to be entered into a computer for processing.

Size is not important: networks are not drawn to scale.

Unlike bar charts, precedence diagrams are not drawn to any timescale. Neither the size of the boxes nor the lengths of the arrows matters at all. But remember that the succession of tasks always goes from left to right. Always!

Any activity which takes time, or which could hold up progress, should be included as a task on the network diagram. So, for example, waiting for concrete to cure or for paint to dry is called a task in a precedence diagram, even though no actual work or cost is involved. Here the time needed is the important factor, because it delays following tasks. If the client or an inspector has to approve a drawing or some site work before the next task can start, that should also be included as a task on the network, even if we think that the approval will be almost immediate and certain. The point here is that if the 'task' is not finished (in other words, if we do not get approval), no following tasks can be started and the project will be held up.

In practice we need to show more information in the boxes. In particular, we must show all the time information. This is especially important because the diagrams are not drawn to scale and we have to rely on day numbers or dates written on the chart to put the project into its timeframe. Figure 3.2 shows the preferred method for drawing a task box, complete with all time data for the task. The way in which the times are calculated will be explained later in this chapter.

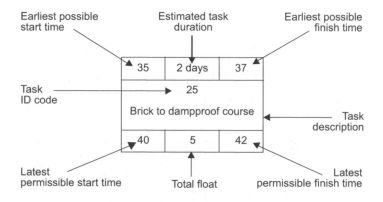

Think of networks as a way of writing down our planning thoughts – like a language. Every language has its rules for vocabulary and grammar. If we ignore those rules no one will be able to understand what we write or say.

Figure 3.2 *Conventional layout for a task box in a precedence diagram*

The convention shown in Figure 3.2 applies especially to network diagrams drawn by hand because it provides spaces for us to write in all the times for each task as we do our calculations (called time analysis). But when computers plot networks, the amount of information that can be shown in the task boxes is very limited. If the computer program tried to stick to the convention shown in Figure 3.2, the activity boxes would have to be so large that only a few could be seen on the screen at the same time. To see and check the network diagram for a project with hundreds of different tasks would mean too much scrolling up, down and sideways. Worse still, the network plots from the printer would be very, very big. Too big, in fact.

Every project management software designer has his or her own ideas about how much to show in each task box. Many computer programs let the project manager or planner customize the boxes, so that they can either show a lot of detail or just a little. When the time comes to use the computer, we must look to reports printed out as tabulations if we want to get the full picture of all possible times for every task. The use of computers will be explained briefly in Chapter 6.

Now we have a system for writing down the sequence of tasks in a project, and showing how the start of each task depends on other tasks being finished first. Although a linked bar chart could do the same thing, the precedence diagram clearly does the job better and is far easier to follow.

Practical ways of sketching precedence network diagrams

All projects, of course, have more than six tasks, and all real precedence diagrams are much bigger than the one shown in Figure 3.1. Sketching a fairly complicated pattern of tasks can be a tedious and time-consuming job. On medium- to large-sized projects, one or more planning meetings are often held, with all the key managers and supervisors present to help the planner draw the initial chart. The presence of such highly experienced people in the planning meeting helps to ensure that no task is forgotten and that the sequence on the chart is the best for all concerned.

Two heads are better than one but, for a planning meeting, six would be better still.

An important point here is that if all the supervisors and managers have helped to draw the plan, they should be more willing to agree to follow the plan when the time comes to do the work. The more time and thought that can be given to this process of drawing the network logic the better. Planning meetings usually brew up a lot of discussion and argument about the best way to go about building the project. The planner should be prepared, without complaining, to alter the plan many times as the meeting progresses and the collective ideas gel. So soft pencils and erasers are the order of the day. Pens are not needed and should be kept well out of sight. The plan that emerges should be a valuable consensus, using the expertise of all those present and faithfully recording their collective ideas.

Time taken at planning meetings is very precious because managers, supervisors and perhaps senior designers or engineers need to be present. We are looking at an expensive gathering of people, and every minute will cost a lot of money. Planning meetings often last several hours so they don't come cheap. So we need to start the meetings on time and manage them so that no time is wasted. The meeting members should not be expected to wait while the planner takes great pains to draw each task box with nitpicking care. Yet that drawing must be done somehow if each box is to look like the one shown in Figure 3.2. Otherwise there would be nowhere to write all the numbers when we do the time calculations. So we must find some way of sketching the diagram quickly but neatly, complete with the task boxes. We should start with a sheet or roll of paper large enough to carry all the information in one piece so that it can all be seen as a whole diagram. This can be laid out on a reference table but it's better if it's hung along a wall. Flipcharts are sometimes used, but they are really far too small.

We could have a rubber stamp specially made for a task box, complete with all its internal lines. Whenever someone at the meeting says we need a task for this or that, the planner can then simply plonk down the stamp at the appropriate place on the paper. But that has the disadvantage of finality. Once plonked, the tasks cannot be unplonked. We really need a method that allows for erasing and changing the pattern as the plan is talked through.

One popular method is to use 3M Post-it® notes, and there is no reason why each of these should not be preprinted with the task box and all its internal lines. That method is fine provided that all the sticky notes stay stuck, and don't get moved when the plan is rolled up and carried away after the meeting to be transferred to a more permanent home, such as a computer memory.

Yet another solution, if a drawing office and printer are available, is to prepare a pattern of task boxes on a roll or very large sheet of paper in a regular grid pattern before the meeting. This leaves the planner free to choose and use only those boxes that fall into the right places during the planning session. This idea, which I have used myself, is illustrated (in miniature) in Figure 3.3.

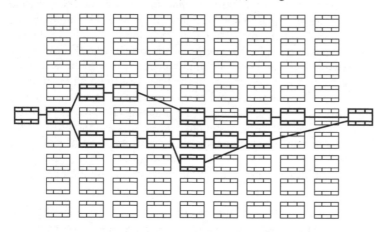

Figure 3.3 *A template guide to help in sketching a small draft network*

Then, of course, there are many project management computer programs that allow precedence network diagrams to be drawn directly on the screen. But the computer method has serious limitations for drawing networks directly because only a few activities can be shown on the screen at the same time, unless they are zoomed out to the point where the data are completely unreadable. So a large sheet or roll of paper is best, at least for the first sketch. The computer can come later.

Milestones

During the process of identifying all the different tasks and putting them into their preferred sequence, some thought should be given to picking out those tasks that have particular significance for the project. For example, the day when the plans have been approved, the time when work starts on site, the instant when the roof is made weatherproof are key events. We call the tasks associated with these particularly important events *milestones*. We need to highlight milestones on the network chart and usually do this by putting a

Milestones help to mark the way on a planning journey.

letter M or an inverted triangle over the box. The start of the project and its finish are the two most obvious milestones.

Later, if the plan is processed by computer, cost and progress reports can be produced for senior management that contain only the milestones, leaving out the many items of data that need not concern them.

Adding the dimension of time to the network

Time units

Now we come to the question of time. Before starting to make any time estimate or calculate any calendar dates we must decide whether to plan using days, weeks or months. The choice depends to some extent on the kind and size of the project. For instance, it would not be very clever to make all the time estimates in minutes for a project expected to last for two years. If the project is fairly small, you might try starting with units of one half-day. Then, if there are five working days in a week, ten plan units will be equal to one week. A very common choice, and the default assumption of many computer programs, uses whole days, with five days equivalent to one calendar week.

It is best practice and, usually essential, to use a common unit of time throughout a network plan. Although it is possible to mix perhaps days and hours in the same plan (if using Microsoft Project software, for instance), this can lead to some very messy output reports that no self-respecting project manager would want others to see.

If we choose weekdays as our planning time units, all initial plans will have to be expressed as day numbers, and the results will have to stay as day numbers until the start date of the project is known. Conversion to calendar dates will, of course, be needed before actual work starts but that difficult calculation can safely be left to a computer.

Estimating task durations

How long is a piece of string? The project planner must know how to estimate times.

For critical path networks, every time estimate should be the best opinion of how long each task should take, measured in the units of the network (days will be used throughout this book). The time expected to pass between the start of a job and its finish is referred to as the elapsed time or, more usually, the *task duration*.

Each time estimate is not directly connected with the work content as measured in man-hours or cost. A job estimated to take five days might need one, two, or more people but, for the purposes of the critical path network, it is the five days' duration that is important.

We have to follow some common-sense rules in this respect. Suppose that a task could best be done by two electricians working together for four days. If the planner knows that at least two electricians are usually available, then that task duration should certainly be estimated as four days. At this stage the planner need not be concerned that other tasks in the project might also need those electricians at the same time. That problem can be solved later, in a calculation known as resource scheduling (explained in the next chapter).

Don't try to do too much too soon. Make the duration estimates first. Worry about the resources later.

Time analysis

When the precedence network has been drawn and all the duration estimates have been made we can work out some important times. These include:

- how long the project should take to finish
- when each task should be done
- which tasks must have priority if resources are scarce and have to be shared between jobs.

These calculations are always called *time analysis*. A very small project network is all we need to demonstrate simply how this is done and Project Simple, introduced in Figure 3.1, is quite big enough for this purpose.

The network for Project Simple shown in Figure 3.4 has been changed so that it conforms to the conventional layout for the task boxes. You will notice that the duration for every task has been estimated and entered on the chart. These estimates are in days for this project, with five days in a working week.

Choose a suitable time unit, such as days, and then always use the same units in all your plans.

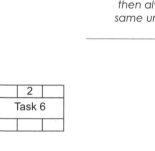

Figure 3.4 *Simple project network with task duration estimates added*

The forward pass

The first thing that any project manager wants to know after the network has been drawn and all the task durations have been estimated is how long the project is likely to take from start to finish. This is calculated by adding up all the activity durations in the network, remembering that the action always flows from left to right. This is not quite as straightforward as you might think, because there is always more than one path through the network from project start to finish.

The forward pass finds the earliest possible times for all tasks in the network.

Figure 3.5 shows how the task durations should be added up during the left-to-right pass through the network. This is always called the forward pass. The forward pass results are written in the spaces at the top of each task box, using the convention already given in Figure 3.2.

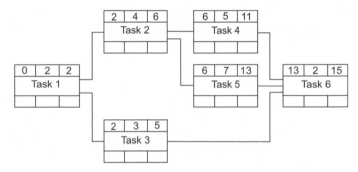

Figure 3.5 *Simple project network after the forward pass*

The first question is, what is the earliest possible start for task 1? Well, we don't yet know the actual date when this project will start, but what is certain is that task 1 will come first. So the earliest possible start for task 1 is right at the start of the project, which is always called day 0. That result is written in the top left-hand corner of the box for task 1.

The earliest possible finish time for a task is its earliest possible start time plus its estimated duration.

The next question is, if task 1 can start at day 0, what is its earliest possible finish time? The duration of this task has been estimated as two days, so if the job is started at day 0 it can be finished by day 2. This actually means close of work on day 1, leaving the next task ready to start at the beginning of day 2.

Once task 1 has been finished, tasks 2 and 3 can start. The earliest possible start time for both activities 2 and 3 is therefore at the beginning of day 2. So we can write 2 in the top left-hand space in each of these task boxes. Then, continuing from left to right, it is clear that the earliest possible finish time for task 2 will be the start of day 6, and the earliest finish time for task 3 must be the beginning of day 5. So the planner must continue to add up all the times from left to right until the earliest times for task 6 are found.

Notice that three tasks lead into task 6. Task 6 cannot start until tasks 3, 4 and 5 have all been finished. Task 6 therefore cannot start until the beginning of day 13. Now the planner knows that the earliest possible finish time for this final task, and for Project Simple, is day 15 (the earliest start time for task 6 plus its duration). Day 15 here means the start of work on day 15, which to all intents and purposes is the same as close of work on day 14.

Day and night – computer style

Computers often do irritating and unexpected things, but sometimes the results are amusing. In a project where a task has been estimated with zero duration, the computer will show that task seeming to finish on the day before it starts. Why would it do that, you may ask? Well, remember that the close of work on one day is (in plan time) the same instant as the start of work on the next day. That is because, in the time available for project work, the night hours simply don't exist. They are invisible to the computer. If weekend days are non-working (as they usually are) then the results can be a bit weird. The computer's default calendar will plan using only the hours available between 08.00 and 17.00 on each of the five weekdays. It will ignore all the out-of-hours time that passes between close of work on each Friday evening and start of work on the following Monday morning. That, if I've done my sums right, is 61 'lost' hours. So the computer might schedule a job with an estimated duration of zero (such as 'project handover') to start on a Monday morning but finish on the previous Friday evening. Now that's creepy.

Not a venture into the paranormal, but merely a quirk of the computer.

The backward pass

The forward pass has answered the question 'What is the earliest possible time in which Project Simple could be finished?'. The next question is 'If this project could be finished by the beginning of day 15, what is its *latest permissible* finish time?'.

The backward pass finds the critical path and the latest permissible times for all the tasks.

Human nature and business pressures being what they are, the answer will usually be that the project finish is wanted now or even yesterday. So the earliest possible finish time will also be the latest permissible finish time. The latest permissible time for task 6 is therefore the beginning of day 15, and this result is written in the bottom right-hand corner of the task box. This begins the backward pass through the network, from right to left, to arrive at the fully annotated network shown in Figure 3.6.

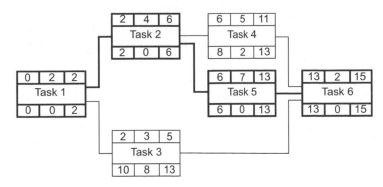

Figure 3.6 *Simple project network after the backward pass*

Now comes another question. If the latest permissible *finish* time for task 6 is day 15, what is its latest permissible *start* date? Because the estimated duration of task 6 is two days, it cannot be allowed to start later than day 15 minus 2, which is day 13. According to the convention shown in Figure 3.2 the latest start time (day 13) must be written in the bottom left-hand corner of the box for task 6.

The latest permissible start time for a task is its latest permissible finish time minus the task duration.

If each task is examined in turn, starting from the project finish at the right-hand side, and working from right to left (backwards) through the network, the latest permissible start and finish times can be calculated for each task. Look at task 2 in Figure 3.6, for example. That task is followed by tasks 4 and 5. Note that the latest permissible start time for task 4 is day 8 (13 − 5) and for task 5 it is day 6 (13 − 7). So, working backwards, we must choose whether day 6 or day 8 is the latest permissible finish time for task 2. Of course it must be day 6 because, if task 2 finished any later, task 5 could not start on day 6.

So, when working backwards, the latest permissible finish time for any task must be the latest permissible start time for the next task. If there is more than one task following immediately afterwards (in other words, if the path branches), the earliest of the possible results must be used. Otherwise one or more of the following tasks could not start until after its latest permissible time.

Float and the critical path

For the ordinary planner in the street there is no real difference between the words 'slack' and 'float'. Most Americans use 'slack', and British managers usually use 'float'.

Look at task 3 in Figure 3.6. Notice that there is a difference of eight working days between the earliest dates and the latest dates. So the start of task 3, although it could take place on day 2, could be delayed to day 10 without holding up the following task 6. This difference between the earliest and latest times for any task is called the slack or the float. So it can be said that task 3 has a float of eight days. That figure has been written in the box at the centre of the bottom row.

Likewise, the start and finish of task 4 could be delayed, in this case by two days, without delaying task 6. So task 4 has a float of two days, which again is written in the middle of the bottom row of figures.

In all networks, when the forward and backward passes have been done, there will always be at least one path joining tasks whose earliest possible dates are the same as their latest permissible dates. None of these tasks has any float or, to be a little more precise, they all have zero float. In other words, if any of these particular tasks should be delayed, following tasks will also be delayed and the project will be finished late. These tasks are critical to finishing the project on time, so they are called critical tasks and the path joining them is always called the critical path. Sometimes there will be two or more such paths, and a path can branch.

Float (or the lack of it) is very important for project management. Any delay to a task with zero float (a task on the critical path) must delay the project finish and handover. The project manager will therefore want to give most attention and priority to critical tasks when watching progress or allocating scarce resources.

Tasks with the least float demand the greatest management attention and must have priority when scarce resources are allocated.

There are implications if a task near the beginning of the path is delayed. For example, when two or more tasks having some float lie on the same path through the network, not only will that task lose an amount of float equal to the delay but the loss of float will be felt right along the path. Imagine four tasks lying one after another on the same path, and suppose that these tasks each have five days' float. If the first of the four tasks is delayed by two days, then the float of the three following activities will also be reduced by two days to only three days. The float in this case is called *total float*, because it is a total amount shared along several activities. Most float in a typical network is total float.

Total float is the difference between the earliest possible start time for a task and the latest permissible start time. This is the same as the difference between the earliest possible finish time and the latest permissible finish time.

If all the tasks in a particular path actually do take place at their earliest times, they will have used none of the total float, and now all that float is left to the last activity in the path. At this point, it becomes known as *free float*, because if it is used up it will not affect the earliest starts of the task's following activities. We shall see some examples of free float when we look at the critical path analysis for the workshop project, which follows.

Free float occurs at a task when the immediately preceding tasks have taken place at their earliest possible times and the immediately following tasks can still take place at their earliest times. Free float is not very common.

Precedence network for the workshop project

Figure 3.7 (see pages 34–5) shows the precedence network diagram for the workshop building project that was introduced in Chapter 2. This time, unlike the bar charts in Figures 2.2 and 2.3, I have taken a little more care to get the logic right and have included the final task of clearing the site and getting rid of the skips.

It is never easy to show a plan of any realistic size on the small page of a book and even this small network, with only 25 separate tasks in the plan, spreads over two pages. But although we have to keep the example simple, this small project network shows all the more important features of the precedence critical path method. Although a project of this size could be managed without a critical path network, larger projects are a different story. But we can only demonstrate the method here using a small project. So, what can this plan tell us?

What the network diagram cannot tell us

Let's start by looking at things that the plan can't tell us. There are four important points here:

1   Until we know the start date for the project, we can only plan in day numbers whereas in practice we need calendar dates.
2   There is no thought of resources, of how many people will be needed each day, or whether there will be too many people on some days and not enough on others.
3   Limited space on the diagram (and on later computer reports) usually means that we have to abbreviate the descriptions or names of tasks, sometimes very severely. All planners become good at describing jobs with as few words as possible. So we would 'dig founds' rather than 'excavate the foundations' for example.
4   The network diagram in Figure 3.7, as it stands, is of no use at all in the day-to-day allocation of jobs or measuring progress. Give it to the site foreman or manager of the workshop project and it would be returned pretty smartly along with a few well chosen words, most of them only four letters long and some of which you might never have heard before.

A picture is worth 1000 words – but a critical path network needs 1000 words to explain it.

Now remember that planning is a logical process that must be done in a series of practicable steps. A mathematician, if you should happen to know one, would tell you that any problem with a lot of unknown quantities has to be solved by eliminating the variables one at a time. There is a sensible number of steps for solving all the variables to make a full project plan. I shall list all these steps in Chapter 5, which deals with planning larger projects.

In practice, we can use a computer for time analysis and, if we need it, for resource scheduling too. The computer is a very convenient tool for printing out work-to-do lists and, once we give it the start date for our project, all these schedules will come out with meaningful calendar dates instead of useless day numbers.

The network diagram is, therefore, just one step in the planning process. By itself it has no use. But it is a valuable means to an end, and gives us useful information which we can use to make a practical schedule.

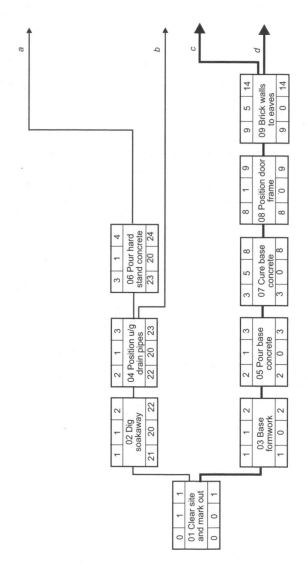

Figure 3.7 *Precedence network diagram for the workshop project. All times are estimated in days*

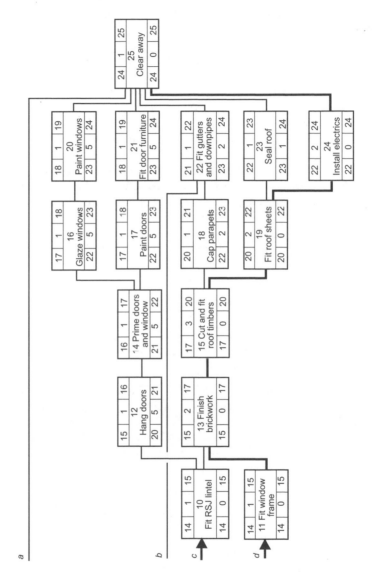

Figure 3.7 Concluded

What the network diagram can tell us

There is a lot of information about the small workshop project in the simple network diagram shown in Figure 3.7. From that diagram we can learn:

- the earliest possible completion time for the project
- the earliest possible start and finish times for each task
- the latest permissible start and finish times for each task
- that tasks 01, 03, 05, 07, 08, 09, 10, 11, 13, 15, 19, 24 and 25 are all on the critical path, with zero float. Any delay in finishing one of these tasks would delay the project finish.

The network diagram gives essential information for input to the computer. Further, it lets us or the computer concentrate on allocating scarce resources to the tasks that are critical or have the least float.

Analysing and tabulating the time analysis results for the workshop project

Review of the time analysis calculations

Now look, for example, at the final task in the network in Figure 3.7, which is task 25. Note how the earliest start and finish times have been calculated for this task.

Task 25 cannot begin until tasks 06, 20, 21, 22, 23 and 24 have all been finished. So the forward pass reveals that task 24, which cannot finish until day 24, will fix the earliest possible start for task 25. So, we write 24 in the top left-hand box of task 25. Then the earliest possible finish for task 25, because it is estimated to take one day, is 24 + 1, which is day 25.

Now go to task 15. The latest permissible finish time for this task must be found by the right-to-left (backward) pass through the network. There are two tasks immediately following task 15. Task 18 has a latest start time of day 22, and task 19 must start by day 20. So task 19 sets the latest finish for task 15, because it would delay the start of task 19 if it finished later than day 20. Day 20 is the latest permissible finish time for task 15.

All tasks where the latest and earliest dates are the same have zero float and are critical. The critical path is marked in this network diagram by the bold link lines. Notice that the critical path branches to take in both task 10 and task 11. Such branching is quite common in network diagrams.

Now look at the line of four tasks 12, 14, 17 and 21. There is a total float of five days shared by all these tasks. This means that, if the finish of task 12 should be (say) two days late, the float among activities 14, 17 and 21 would be reduced to three days if the project is still to finish by day 25. Task 21, at the end of this line is a little different. If all its preceding tasks are done on time, then it will still have five days float left. And if task 21 should be up to five days late in finishing, no other task start would be affected. So we can say that task 21 has a free float of five days. There is no space on the network diagram to write in this free float, but we can do that by putting all the results in a table (Table 3.1).

Task ID	Task description	Duration (days)	Earliest start	Earliest finish	Latest start	Latest finish	Free float	Total float
01	Clear site and mark out	1	0	1	0	1	0	0
02	Dig soakaway and trench	1	1	2	21	22	0	20
03	Base formwork	1	1	2	1	2	0	0
04	Position underground pipes	1	2	3	22	23	0	20
05	Pour base concrete	1	2	3	2	3	0	0
06	Pour hard standing for cars	1	3	4	23	24	20	20
07	Cure base concrete	5	3	8	3	8	0	0
08	Position door frame	1	8	9	8	9	0	0
09	Brick walls to eaves	5	9	14	9	14	0	0
10	Fit RSJ lintel	1	14	15	14	15	0	0
11	Fit window frame	1	14	15	14	15	0	0
12	Hang doors	1	15	16	20	21	0	5
13	Finish brickwork	2	15	17	15	17	0	0
14	Prime doors and window	1	16	17	21	22	0	5
15	Cut and fit roof timbers	3	17	20	17	20	0	0
16	Glaze windows	1	17	18	22	23	0	5
17	Paint doors	1	17	18	22	23	0	5
18	Cap parapets	1	20	21	22	23	0	2
19	Fit roof sheets	2	20	22	20	22	0	0
20	Paint window frame	1	18	19	23	24	5	5
21	Fit door furniture	1	18	19	23	24	5	5
22	Fit gutters and downpipes	1	21	22	23	24	2	2
23	Seal roof	1	22	23	23	24	1	1
24	Install electrics	2	22	24	22	24	0	0
25	Clear away site and skips	1	24	25	24	25	0	0

Table 3.1 Time analysis results for the workshop project

The tabulation of time analysis results for the workshop project is given in Table 3.1. The layout is a standard format used by many project managers. Most project management computer software can produce such tables.

Without the computer, our tabulation is still based on day numbers. Once the computer has processed the network data, however, this table can be printed with calendar dates and, at last, (ignoring the question of resources for the moment) we will have a very useful working schedule for the workshop project.

Dangles and loops

No, this is not about trendy jewellery. There is nothing pretty about dangles and a loop can put paid to your time analysis or even stop your computer in its tracks. Dangles and loops are traps for beginners, but even the most expert planners can be fooled by them. Take a look at Figure 3.8 and all will be explained.

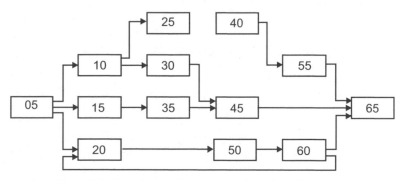

Figure 3.8 *Dangles and loops (errors in network logic)*

Figure 3.8 shows the outline of a small network diagram. The network may be small, but it has more than its fair share of mistakes. Note that the planner has forgotten to put in the link from the finish of task 25 to the start of task 40. This means that, to all intents and purposes, task 25 is at the end of a path and task 40 is at the start of another. In the colourful language of network analysis, task 25 is called an end dangle (because it has been left dangling, with nowhere to go). Task 40 is a start dangle. Dangles like these are often caused when planners forget to specify a link between activities when they first enter data into the computer. Dangles ruin time analysis because they prevent complete forward and backward passes from the start to finish of the whole network.

Loops can trip you up, and dangles might lead you astray.

Now look at task 60 in Figure 3.8. The planner had intended to take the arrow from this task to the start of task 65, but she or he has made a mistake. The arrow leading out of task 60 has mistakenly been taken back to the start of task 20. Such a mistake is unlikely to be made when drawing the network but, especially if the ID codes are complicated, it is easy for someone to type a wrong number into the computer that will create a mistake like this. The result is a continuous loop around tasks 20, 50 and 60. Imagine what the computer would do when trying to calculate times in the forward and backward passes in this network. It would have no chance and would have to give up, stop and cry for help.

Even experts make these mistakes. I once had a very experienced assistant who had drawn a 1200 task network on a long roll of paper. We had enormous drawing boards for that purpose in that office. He was busy writing in the task ID codes, from left to right when, halfway through this job, he was interrupted by a telephone call. When he got back to his work he had forgotten the last number entered. He duplicated about 50 task numbers (that is, he gave about 50 tasks in different parts of this big network duplicate ID codes). In due course this project was entered into a computer for time analysis and resource allocation. The result was a great heap of paper from the printer listing hundreds of errors that took two of us days to sort out.

You might wonder why the task ID codes in Figure 3.8 step up in fives. Why weren't the tasks numbered simply 1, 2, 3, 4 and so on? Well, although it is not necessary for these numbers to increase steadily from left to right, it is convenient if they do because then it is easy to find a task on a large network drawing if we know its ID code. If the ID codes were jumbled, with high and low numbers mixed throughout the network, we might spend ages looking for a task with a particular ID code on the diagram. So we always try to increase the ID codes steadily from left to right. But network diagrams are often changed as the project proceeds. If we had not left gaps in the ID code sequence, any new tasks inserted into the plan would have to be given ID codes that were out of step. This would not matter to the computer, but it helps us as mere humans if we can slot in new tasks with their ID codes still kept in sequence.

Complex links in precedence network diagrams

There are times in projects when we do not have to wait for one task to finish completely before the next task can start. For example, purchasing and other work on a project can often start before all the design has been finished.

Precedence network diagrams allow the planner to show complex links between tasks, so that (for example) the start of one task is not necessarily dependent on the predecessor task being completely finished. None of the examples in this book uses these complex links, and they are not used as often in real life as the straightforward finish-start links. However, they can be very useful in some circumstances, so they are illustrated here in Figure 3.9.

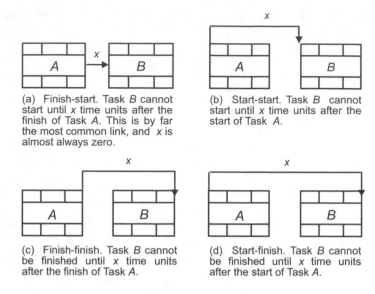

(a) Finish-start. Task B cannot start until x time units after the finish of Task A. This is by far the most common link, and x is almost always zero.

(b) Start-start. Task B cannot start until x time units after the start of Task A.

(c) Finish-finish. Task B cannot be finished until x time units after the finish of Task A.

(d) Start-finish. Task B cannot be finished until x time units after the start of Task A.

Figure 3.9 *Complex links between tasks in precedence networks*

All project management computer software will assume that no task can start before every predecessor has been completely finished, which is another way of saying that all links between consecutive tasks are of the finish-start kind unless the planner chooses to instruct the computer to the contrary. Yet another way of putting this is that all links between consecutive tasks are assumed to be finish-start by default. Most programs will, however, allow the planner to specify complex links where these are considered to be appropriate.

When using complex links, special care has to be taken not to create dangles. For example, a start-start link will usually also mean giving the two consecutive tasks a finish-finish link. Otherwise the first task would become an end dangle. You can see how this might happen if you look at Figure 3.9(a).

Chapter **4**

Scheduling Project Resources

Because this chapter is all about resources, it might be best to start by explaining exactly what project resources are. Then we can decide which resources can be scheduled and list some of those that are difficult, or even impossible, to schedule. Next we have to decide whether or not we want to schedule resources at all. Finally, if we do need to schedule resources, we can consider how to go about it.

Three kinds of project resource

Resources can usually be labelled in one of three ways:

1 exhaustible
2 replaceable
3 re-usable.

Exhaustible resources

Coal, oil, natural gas and other substances that we get from the Earth are exhaustible resources. Once they have been used up, they have been used up and that's that. But let's hope they will last out for our lifetime and for our projects. So, as far as we project managers are concerned, we can shift these into another category, replaceable resources, which are described next. But (and, if you'll pardon the expression, it's a very big BUT) there is one truly exhaustible resource that we must never ignore. That resource is TIME. Unless you believe in the paranormal, or are an exceptionally gifted cosmic scientist, you must agree that once a particular moment in time has passed it really is dead and gone and we shall never see its like again. So, if we have promised to hand over a building for occupation on 31 October and it is now 1 November and the roof is not yet on, the project is late and there's nothing we can do about it (except perhaps to think up some good excuses or possibly placate the project purchaser with a plentiful pile of pricey presents).

Time (and tide) wait for no man. So why can't we have more women project managers?

Replaceable resources

Most materials used on site are replaceable if they get used up, damaged, lost or stolen. Bulk materials such as bricks, sand, cement, ballast, rebar and so on are replaceable. So if these materials should run short, no problem, just order some more. Items supplied specially under contract, such as structural steel and air-conditioning equipment, are also replaceable, although it might take a little more time to get the replacements.

Money is a replaceable resource. When your bank account is heavily in the red and all your suppliers are pressing for payment whilst your customers owe you £100 000, money might not be the first thing that comes to mind when talking about replaceable

Money is often a replaceable resource because the banks might be willing to bail out a project to stop it sinking with all its sunk costs on board.

resources. But just think: if you owe your bank £200 000 against an unsecured overdraft and need to borrow only £10 000 more to finish a £1 million project, do you think that your bank would refuse and foreclose? All the money that you have spent to date on this project is best described as sunk costs. If the bank lends you the further £10 000 you can finish your project and pay back the whole overdraft. If you go bust, the bank simply becomes one of your creditors at your bankruptcy hearing and it would be lucky to see a fraction of its money back. There have been many projects where banks have forked out more cash to avoid seeing the project and all its sunk costs sink without trace.

Re-usable resources

Re-usable resources can be used on more than one project. Home office space and equipment are re-usable resources. People and most hire plant are obvious re-usable resources. When one job ends, these resources can be moved on to be used somewhere else. Hire plant can be returned to the hirer. People can be moved to other work, or 'let go' to retire or find new employment.

Re-usable resources are like catalysts in chemical reactions. They are necessary for the reaction to happen but themselves remain unchanged at the end. Of course this is not an exact analogy, because hire plant will wear out in time and not all people finish work on a project completely unchanged (because of accidents or the ravages of old age). Nevertheless we have to presume that some resources are re-usable and can be scheduled for allocation to one job after another.

Resources that can, or cannot, be scheduled

To schedule any resource we need to know several things. I was going to say several facts, but in planning we are really talking about forecasts or inspired guesses rather than facts. Anyway, here are the things we need to know:

1 What kind of resource are we considering (electrician, crane, plumber, bricks)?
2 What tasks is the resource to be used on?
3 When will the resource be needed for each task (task start time, duration and finish)?
4 At what rate will the resource be used on the task (how much or how many per day)?
5 How many people of each resource type will be available when they are needed?
6 What happens if other projects that we are doing need the same resources at the same time?

Planning, estimating and the use of the computer can eventually answer all of these questions provided that we can put a simple number on the amount of the resource needed and we are using good project management software. Thus we can schedule electricians, for example, because we can use simple numbers to define the quantity.

There are a few kinds of resource that cannot be specified by simple numbers. These are practically impossible to schedule with project management computer systems. Space is the most common example, because we are often concerned not only with the area in square feet or square metres, but also the shape of the space and things such as access, the clearance height needed or position relative to a crane. Space of this kind can be scheduled, but it needs special software more related to computer-aided design rather than project management software.

We should note here that resource scheduling methods can also schedule costs for us, provided that we know how to use the project management software correctly. We do this because money can be specified as a resource and quantified in the units of currency that apply to our project. This aspect of resource scheduling is not for beginners but, with some experience, it is possible to estimate some costs and even produce forecasts of net cash flow schedules.

Good project management software can schedule any resource provided it can be quantified in simple single dimensional units (such as fitters, joiners, Euros, metres and so on).

Do we really need to schedule any resources?

Circumstances where resource scheduling might not be needed

If you are a tiny company, perhaps employing yourself and one or two helpers, then your projects are going to be fairly simple and you can probably do all your resource scheduling mentally or in a diary. You will 'muddle through' quite happily from day to day and change your plans to suit illness, the weather and other difficulties as they arise. You can get along fine without using project management software to do your resource scheduling. The process is intuitive, is not to be sneered at, and relies on your experience with past projects and common sense.

Now, suppose you use subcontractors for all the trades on site. So, apart from a site foreman and the odd labourer, you employ no direct labour. For you, resource scheduling should be no problem. You will need a plan to set the timeframe for all the different tasks. But for resource scheduling all you need to do is to agree (preferably in a written contract) with each subcontractor what has to be done, what it will cost, the terms of payment, when the job should start and when you want it to finish. Your subcontractors must then produce their own work schedules to suit your project. So they will do all the resource scheduling because they will have to find all the direct labour needed.

If you are a self-employed one-man band or if you use subcontractors for all your trades on site, you probably don't need any clever resource scheduling methods. You might even want to skip the rest of this chapter. But perhaps you should skim through it, just in case there's something here for you.

Circumstances where resource scheduling must be considered or is essential

If your company employs direct labour for construction, either as a main contractor or as a subcontractor, then those people who we rather unkindly call 'direct labour' need to be scheduled. Provided that you can draw a critical path network diagram to plan the work, you should be able to use project management software to make schedules with a fairly smooth workload.

If you have a large head office staff, perhaps as a managing contractor or as a large subcontracting company, you will need to schedule your head office staff resources. These resources might include architects, designers, civil and structural engineers, heating and ventilating engineers and so on. Your head office staff will probably be working on more than one project at the same time, so you will have to get involved in multi-project scheduling (Chapter 6) and you will need to know something about project organization structures (Chapter 7).

Benefits of resource scheduling

For anyone employing direct labour, resource scheduling is not a luxury or simply something that is nice to have. It can cut costs, use people's time better and speed up your projects.

Companies that ask their senior staff to plan all their significant projects using critical path networks are more likely to use the most efficient processes and working practices. When good project management software is also used to schedule the resources, workloads are smoother, there are fewer panics and bottlenecks, and less idle time. All of this improves motivation, speeds up project completion and reduces costs, especially when all the projects in the organization are put into the resource scheduling calculation. I have seen companies on both sides of the Atlantic make very significant improvements (over 20 per cent) in their performance as a result of multi-project resource scheduling using computers, and starting from carefully drawn critical path networks.

Making a start

Naming and quantifying the resources to be scheduled

Start by choosing which resources you need to schedule. It is not necessary or usual to try to schedule the time of supervisors and managers – they plan their own time using their diaries. Try to decide which kind or kinds of resource you use and depend on most to get your project work done. Don't try to schedule more than about four different kinds of resource, at least to begin with. Then for each kind of resource you have chosen you will need to prepare some basic information for the computer. Suppose you work for a large company and want to schedule design engineers in a head office department. You would need, as a minimum, to have the following information ready:

Permanent staff in a head office department will not all be available for work on your project all of the time. Some will be ill or on holiday or doing other jobs. So if you have ten design engineers (DE), lie to the computer and tell it that you have only eight.

- the name of the resource – in this case, design engineers
- a short code for the resource – for example, DE
- the number of design engineers you can make available for your project
- the dates between which these engineers will be available
- the standard or average daily cost rate for one design engineer.

Estimating the resources needed for each task

If you know you are going to do' resource scheduling, then the resource estimates can be made when you draw the project network and estimate the task durations. That's the best time, at the planning meeting, because that's when the most expert advice should be at hand.

You should think only of the task being estimated and not worry about the fact that other tasks might need the same resources at the same time. Leave that one for the computer to sort out. Simply make your estimates on the basis of the best number of resources for the job. So if a job could best be done by two plumbers (PB) working together for four days, then your task estimate would be written on the network diagram as 4d, 2PB.

Too many cooks spoil the broth, but many hands make light work (unless the fuse has blown).

All good computer programs will let you specify many more than one type of resource for each task. So if, for example, you had a task that needed ten days with four electricians and two plumbers, then you might write 10d, 4EL, 2PB on the network diagram.

Rate constancy

When we say that two plumbers are needed for a job lasting four days, we mean that those two plumbers will be working full-time on that job. That is called a rate constant resource usage. The computer will allocate two plumbers full-time and work out the labour cost for that task as the cost rate per day for one plumber, multiplied by the number of days' duration, multiplied by the number of plumbers.

Now, suppose we have a ten-day job that needs eight labourers (LB), but they are not needed all the time for that job. Perhaps we want to start with two labourers for the first two days, then go to eight labourers for the next five days and then fall back to four labourers for the last three days. Some computer programs will let you specify that pattern. We call it non-rate constant use of resources, or a profiled use of resources. But it's best to try to avoid going to those complicated lengths.

A better solution is to split your task into parts. So in this case you would have one task with two labourers for two days, a separate task for the next five days and a third task for the last three days. Then the estimates for these three parts of the task would be written as 2d, 2LB; 5d, 8LB and 3d, 4LB. I prefer that method because you can see your plan on the network diagram and in the work-to lists that come out of the computer. If you do it all in the software, your decisions are hidden inside the computer and you might forget them. You can label the three separate parts of the task by adding 'Part 1', 'Part 2', 'Part 3' or simply 'A', 'B' and 'C' to the task description.

Scheduling rules

Although we now use computers, some of the principles of modern resource scheduling are the same as those used long ago when all planning and some simple resource scheduling was done using bar charts. So we can use bar charts here to describe those principles.

Resource aggregation

With the old bar chart method we might have coded each task bar with a pattern or colour to show the type of resource needed. For example, a job needing one plumber might have been given a red bar on the chart. If a job needed two or more plumbers, that became more difficult and we would either put two red bars on the chart together or write the number 2 on one red bar.

Suppose each vertical column on our chart represented one working day. Once the plan had been made, we could look down each column on the chart, count up the number of red bars crossing that column, and write down that number as the number of plumbers needed on that day. This is simple addition, with no attempt to smooth the resource usage pattern. We call it resource aggregation. All jobs on bar charts are usually shown at their earliest possible times. So with resource aggregation we are trying to do everything as soon as possible, even though that is not always necessary.

Resource aggregation causes aggravation.

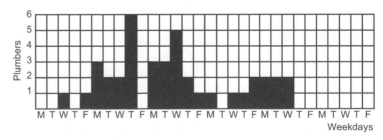

Figure 4.1 *An unsmoothed resource schedule (resource aggregation)*

Figure 4.1 shows a typical pattern that would result from trying to do each job at its earliest possible time. You will agree that this is not a good plan. On one Thursday we appear to need six plumbers but on the next day we don't want any at all. That's a good recipe for upsetting everyone, not least the plumbers. So, resource aggregation is not the ideal solution for resource scheduling. We need to look for something better.

Resource-limited scheduling

Suppose that you have only two plumbers who can work on your project and imagine that your bar chart is set up on an adjustable wallboard that lets you slide the bars sideways (that is, delay some of the jobs) so that you can get rid of the unwanted work overloads and fill the idle troughs. This is a tricky thing to do, because you must always keep the tasks in their correct sequence. But it can be done with a little patience and, if you are lucky, you will finish up with a resource schedule like that shown in Figure 4.2.

Charts like this, which are bar charts turned on their sides, are called histograms.

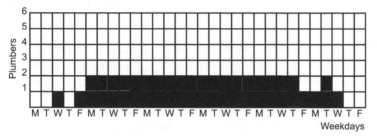

Figure 4.2 *A resource-limited schedule (only two plumbers are available)*

Now we have a splendid schedule, smooth as the proverbial baby's bottom and never needing more than our two plumbers. But it has a snag. The project is now shown as taking five additional working days to finish. So, if we limit the resources used to those that are available there is often a time penalty to pay, which in this case is one calendar week.

Time-limited scheduling

Think what would happen if you went to your client after doing the resource-limited schedule just described and said 'We've only got two plumbers, and that means your project is not going to be ready for you until at least a week later than the contract date'. In fairyland you might get the answer 'Don't fret, I don't mind waiting; I can keep all my new machines and tools under a tarpaulin until the workshop is ready. Just take your time and finish when you can.' But in real life the atmosphere might suddenly get decidedly chilly, with storm clouds gathering, and your client would ask you, perhaps not very politely, to go and find some more plumbers and find them pretty soon.

So if you are going to finish on time, you need more plumbers than the two you already have. You could hire them, but you don't want to go back to the terrible schedule in Figure 4.1. You need a schedule that has been smoothed and which plans to finish the project at its earliest possible time with the least possible additional number of plumbers. The ideal result might look like that in Figure 4.3.

Time-limited schedules use the minimum resources necessary to finish the project on time, but this might mean exceeding the numbers currently available. Some non-critical tasks are put back to reduce overloads but no task is delayed beyond its latest permissible date.

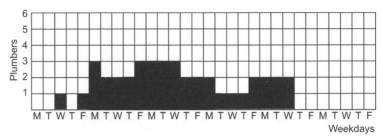

Figure 4.3 *A resource schedule limited by time*

Remaining float is the amount of total float left to a task after its start has been delayed for any reason. Not many people know that. Computers in general are not good at reporting it.

To arrive at a time-limited resource schedule that uses as few extra resources as possible, as smoothly as possible, the following steps need to be followed:

1   start by planning the project with a critical path network
2   carry out time analysis
3   try to start each task at its earliest possible date
4   delay any non-critical task if necessary to move resource usage away from an impossible overload peak, but do not delay any task by more than its remaining float.

This process is very difficult to carry out mentally using an adjustable bar chart. So, even for a small project like the workshop introduced in Chapter 3, we shall have to use a computer. We can try that when we reach Chapter 6.

Chapter 5

Larger and More Complex Plans

So far, the examples in this book have been kept simple so that the diagrams are readable and uncluttered. But, of course, in real life many projects are much larger. A few are very big, with hundreds of companies and thousands of people working on them for many years. This chapter looks at some of the methods used for planning and scheduling these larger projects. If you are a complete newcomer to project management you might find some of the methods explained here somewhat beyond what you need for your own everyday work. These more advanced methods are included to give the complete picture but most of us never have to go to such sophisticated levels of planning. So, if you come to a section in this chapter that seems a little beyond your own project needs, it might then be a good idea to skip to the end of this chapter and read the final part, called 'Putting things into perspective'.

Work breakdown structure (WBS)

In the early days of critical path networks, people used to draw very big networks and boast about the thousands of tasks in them. I've been there myself. I even once saw a network with 10 000 tasks, and of course that was far too big to handle and of little practical use. In more recent times people have become wiser. We recognize that big networks are difficult to deal with. We can't see much of them on the computer screen and, more importantly, no one person can be asked to manage thousands of tasks directly on a day-by-day basis. Enter the idea of the project work breakdown structure, now a popular tool for breaking large projects down into a number of small pieces that can each be handled by one manager, and can more easily be plotted or viewed on a computer screen.

There was once an American project network diagram so big that it had to be drawn in chalk on the floor of an aircraft hangar. When changes had to be made, people shuffled around rubbing out the unwanted lines with their shoes. Copies were made by photographing it with a camera mounted overhead in the steel roof supports.

But unless we are to lose sight of the whole project picture, there must be some logical pattern to the way in which these pieces are broken off. We don't want it to be like smashing a piece of glass into lots of tiny pieces that can't be put back together again. No, we are looking for something more like a jigsaw puzzle, where every piece can be slotted into its right place to make the big picture.

Engineers in manufacturing projects have been using this work breakdown idea for far longer than we have as project managers. When they design a new product (anything from a washing machine to a motor car) they draw a 'goes into chart' or 'family tree' to show how all the bits fit together. The complete product or main assembly sits at the top of the tree, the next rank down contains the subassemblies, there might be another rank below that for sub-sub-assemblies and then, right at the bottom, come all the odd components, fasteners and the like. Every item on the family tree is given a part number, and all those part numbers are related in such a way as to indicate how and where each part fits into the scheme of things.

A project work breakdown structure (WBS) is very similar to a product family tree, with all the parts put into their logical places on

A good WBS is essential for any project of significant size, and forms the basis of many project management procedures and work management aspects.

a tree diagram and given code numbers to identify them and indicate where they fit into the whole project.

For any project of significant size there is usually more than one correct way of drawing the tree. One way is to base the breakdown structure on the physical parts of the project. Another method is more concerned with the organizational pattern and how the work will be allocated to managers and supervisors. Often these two approaches suggest the same breakdown. We can look at a few examples, starting with the simple workshop project that was introduced in Chapter 3.

Two work breakdown examples

WBS for the workshop project

A project as small as the workshop project could be planned without going to the trouble of drawing a WBS chart but if we did decide that a WBS was necessary, the result might look something like the chart shown in Figure 5.1. This version is based on the physical parts of the project, but it does correspond to a large extent with the different trades that will be needed to build the workshop.

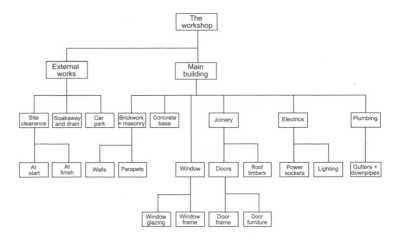

Figure 5.1 *One possible WBS for the workshop project*

WBS for a passenger railway

A work breakdown for a more substantial project is shown in Figure 5.2. Here, a new passenger rail system is to be built across land where no roads or rail existed before. So the route has to be chosen, surveyed and negotiated with many landowners. The project involves many contractors and subcontractors covering every conceivable construction trade, as well as railway specialists.

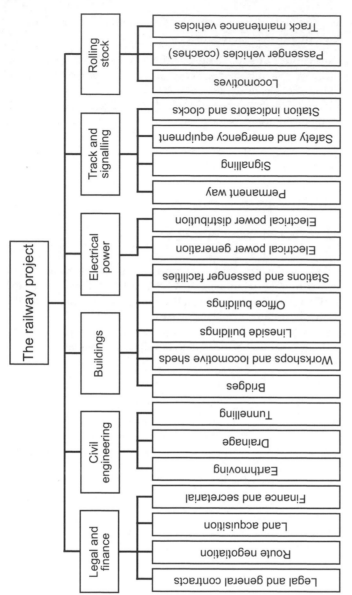

Figure 5.2 Upper levels of the WBS for a project to build a new passenger railway system

This is a good example of a WBS that fits both the physical nature of the project and its organization. We could imagine a board of directors sitting at the top of the chart, in the box marked 'The railway project'. An executive director, senior manager or chief engineer might be appointed for each of the items in the second rank. Then, coming down to the third rank, we could imagine another layer of management so that, for example, one engineer or manager might be given responsibility for designing and building the electrical power generation plant, whilst another person could be put in charge of the permanent way development.

Big fleas have little fleas that sit on 'em and bite 'em. Little fleas have smaller fleas, and so on ad infinitum (after Jonathan Swift, 1667–1745).

Below the items shown on the chart, more levels would take the breakdown further into finer detail. So, under 'Stations and passenger facilities', for example, the next layer of the WBS would have a separate item (and sub-project manager) for each station to be built on the line. This WBS might have many lower levels, each with many more tasks than could possibly be shown here.

This would be a very large project, costing perhaps billions of pounds, and the organization would be huge, employing many different contractors, as well as a large head office staff. Devising a WBS helps those at the top of this project to visualize the project scope more clearly and develop not only the organization but also the overall project schedule.

The main summary schedule for this project would possibly be a network diagram or bar chart listing only the very large tasks. There might be only 50 or 100 tasks in this master schedule, concerned chiefly with the tasks shown in Figure 5.2. Thus a hierarchy of schedules would be developed, with each manager or contractor detailing the schedule of work needed to fit into the overall times determined from the summary plan.

The value of a WBS in a project such as this is inestimable. It is the basis for bottom-up cost estimating, for detailed planning and scheduling, for organizing the project, for setting contractors' and departmental budgets. It makes it possible to deal with the depth of detail needed to issue work, follow up progress and maintain the project on course within its time and cost targets. Without the WBS, no logical pattern for planning and management would exist and the project would be an unprofitable mix of chaos, muddle and panic.

In his eminently practical book Total Project Control (1999, New York, Wiley) Stephen Devaux, obviously writing from experience and from the heart, wrote: 'If I could wish but one thing for every project, it would be a detailed and comprehensive WBS. The lack of a good WBS probably results in more inefficiency, schedule slippage, and cost overruns on projects than any other single cause.'

Introducing a larger project

The UFO Shopping Mall Project

Please imagine that there is a town in the North East of England called Effingham. This is not to be confused with the village of Effingham in Surrey, but is instead a thriving industrial community, twinned with the Dutch town of Blindinghem, and situated about ten miles from Newcastle upon Tyne. The worthy citizens of this town have long complained about their dreary high street and, at last, a well known firm of property developers, the Upkwik and Fawldown Organization (UFO), have been granted planning permission to redevelop a large area in the town centre as a shopping mall, with other amenities. Now please stretch your belief beyond its outer limits and imagine that you have been appointed as project manager for the whole project. How would you make a start? You may take it that the outline

> scheme has been approved and that the scope is well defined. Funding is assured, and all you have to do is start planning and organizing in readiness for work to start.

Large projects such as this are often divided into phases. At least five distinct phases can be identified for the UFO shopping mall project. These are as follows:

- Phase 1: concept, initial designs and a feasibility study.
- Phase 2: discussions with the planning authorities, banks and other stakeholders leading to some design revisions, financing and planning approval.
- Phase 3: detailed design and construction of the main structure and all its internal and external services.
- Phase 4: occupational works carried out by or at the instruction of tenants.
- Phase 5: operation and maintenance of the finished project.

We join this project after the first two phases have been finished. All the explanations and exhibits in this chapter are concerned only with Phase 3 of the project.

WBS and coding system for the UFO shopping mall project

Form of the WBS

You would need to start this project by preparing a WBS. There are several acceptable ways in which the WBS chart might be constructed, and one of these is shown in Figure 5.3. This chart shows only the first three layers of the WBS for this expensive project and, in practice, several more layers of work breakdown would be needed before all the smallest construction jobs and components could be included.

Even at these three summary upper levels, lack of space does not allow every part of the work breakdown to be shown. Thus, at the second level of the chart a few small details such as the infants' crèche, the 15-seater cinema, fitness and leisure centre, three pubs, two supermarkets and a bus station arc missing. At the third level, the external works do not show the essential task of demolishing and clearing away the old existing buildings on the site. All the security systems, access controls, fire alarms and sprinkler systems, environmental controls, automatic lighting systems and so on are lumped together here under 'building management systems'. But our chart is nevertheless sufficiently complete to demonstrate the method.

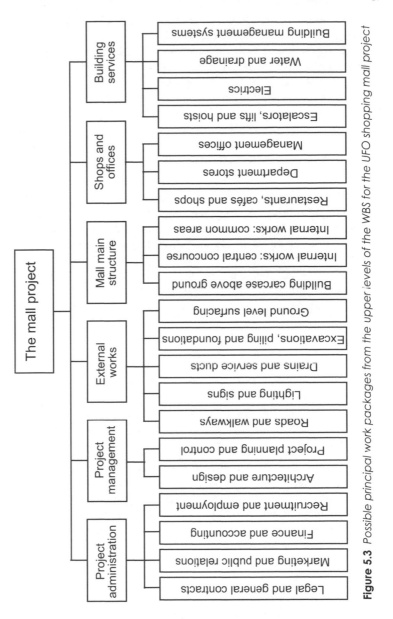

Figure 5.3 *Possible principal work packages from the upper levels of the WBS for the UFO shopping mall project*

Once again, as with the railway project, this is a vast project that could not be planned and managed properly without the WBS, which forms the basis of all the project management systems.

Developing a coding system for the UFO shopping mall project

Coding is an essential part of the work breakdown process in any project. The way in which the coding system is developed is most important and must be given considerable thought. Once decided upon, the coding system must be applied right across all aspects of the project, as a standard from which no exception should be allowed. Every item has to be coded so that the database can file, process, sort, filter, merge and report data to suit the individual needs of the many managers of this project. Each code must identify the particular job, cost or document and indicate where it fits into the hierarchical scheme of things. Yet care must be taken not to overcomplicate the coding system and to avoid codes that include too many characters. So, clearly, the design of a coding system needs a logical, expert approach and is not something to be undertaken lightly.

The local authority has decided to choose a smart name for the shopping mall project. The huge site includes a former plague burial pit and a disused gasworks, but these did not suggest any suitable title. The final choice is to be made from the usual array of fancy appellations such as The Maltings, The Harlequin, The Priory Centre and so on. But, the Upkwik and Fawldown Organization needs a short code name for the project to put at the top of the WBS, and they originally chose UFO-0503. This code was derived as follows:

UFO = Upkwik and Fawldown Organization
05 = 2005, the year in which this project is due to start
03 = the third project out of a maximum possible 99 within the year.

But UFO-0503 is unnecessarily long and complicated. We know that we are working for UFO so we can drop that part of the code. So our main project code can be shortened to 0503.

This means that 0503 is the principal code upon which all the project information will be hung in the main project computer database. It will be the universal prefix to every cost account, specification, contract, purchase order, drawing and job number needed for this project. It can even be preprinted on many project documents as a barcode, to make the lives of those using the codes that little bit easier.

Alphanumeric codes – that is, codes containing both numbers and letters – are generally easier to use and can be arranged to contain more information than simple numeric codes. So if you are wise and treat each item at the second level of this work breakdown as a subproject of your main project, you can simply add a letter suffix to the main project code.

So, based on the WBS in Figure 5.3, things now stand as follows:

Some very clever former colleagues of mine in the mining industry developed a system in which an average code name might be as follows: AN1311-01-04-03-06-115. Logical reasons were argued for needing such long numbers but the practical aspects of engineers (especially Australian engineers) working in all weathers at an exposed Australian mining site had been ignored. So the engineers working on this project simply refused to use these numbers and the system fell apart. Coding systems must be made as simple as possible.

```
Main project code          =        0503
    Subproject codes:
    Project administration  =        0503A
    Project management      =        0503P
    External works          =        0503E
    Mall main structure     =        0503M
    Shops and offices       =        0503S
    Building services       =        0503B
```

The prefix 0503 firmly anchors each of these subprojects to the main project.

Now we have to consider the next level of breakdown. A possible solution for that is given in Figure 5.4. Further development of the coding system is necessary to allocate code numbers to the WBS at the lower levels. Rather than take up a large number of pages in this book with a possible complete arrangement for this project we can take a glimpse at just one of the subprojects. Suppose we look at 0503S, which is 'shops and offices'. The breakdown to the next lower level for this work package might be as shown in Figure 5.5.

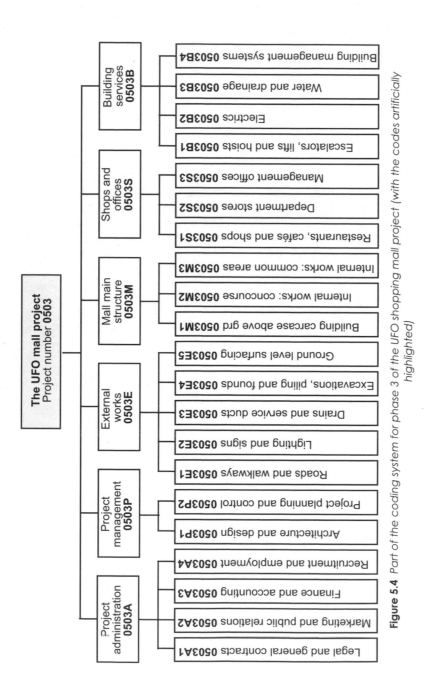

Figure 5.4 Part of the coding system for phase 3 of the UFO shopping mall project (with the codes artificially highlighted)

The UFO mall project
Project number 0503

Project administration 0503A
- Legal and general contracts 0503A1
- Marketing and public relations 0503A2
- Finance and accounting 0503A3
- Recruitment and employment 0503A4

Project management 0503P
- Architecture and design 0503P1
- Project planning and control 0503P2

External works 0503E
- Roads and walkways 0503E1
- Lighting and signs 0503E2
- Drains and service ducts 0503E3
- Excavations, piling and founds 0503E4
- Ground level surfacing 0503E5

Mall main structure 0503M
- Building carcase above grd 0503M1
- Internal works: concourse 0503M2
- Internal works: common areas 0503M3

Shops and offices 0503S
- Restaurants, cafés and shops 0503S1
- Department stores 0503S2
- Management offices 0503S3

Building services 0503B
- Escalators, lifts and hoists 0503B1
- Electrics 0503B2
- Water and drainage 0503B3
- Building management systems 0503B4

Shops and offices 0503S

0503S1	Restaurants, cafés and shops	
	0503S1A	Kate's Carvery
	0503S1B	Bert's Burgers
	0503S1C	Shop unit 01 Faith's Fashions
	0503S1D	Shop unit 02 unlet
	0503S1E	Shop unit 03 unlet
	and so on for 12 more shop units	

0503S2	Department stores	
	0503S2A	Marks and Spencer
	0503S2B	John Lewis
	0503S2C	W.H. Smith
	0503S2D	Army and Navy Stores
	0503S2E	Unlet
	0503S2F	Unlet

0503S3	Management offices	
	0503S3A	Main offices on first floor
	0503S3B	Security office
	0503S3C	First aid room
	0503S3D	Car park office

This is an attempt to keep the coding as simple as possible. The prefix 0503 can be preprinted as a bar code on all relevant project documents.

Figure 5.5 *UFO shopping mall project: example of coding at level 4 of the WBS*

It is usual, and advisable, not to use the letters I and O in codes because these can easily be confused with the numbers one and zero. So that leaves us with 24 possible letters of the alphabet available, which would allow for a combined total of only 24 restaurants, cafés and shop units under 0503S01. However, the mall might contain many more shops than this. We can resolve this little difficulty, without adding another field to the code system, by creating more categories under 0503S. We might, for example, place the ground- and first-floor shop units in two separate categories under 0503S, using 0503S1 for the ground-floor shops and 0503S2 for the first-floor units. Then 0503S3 would be used for the department stores and the management offices would fit under 0503S4. There are, of course, many other simple solutions should the mall have more than the 44 small shop units allowed by the changes suggested here.

Summary of the UFO shopping mall project WBS and its coding

It is useful to stop here for a moment, take a deep breath and think about what we have achieved so far in planning this big project.

When this project first started, it was all chaos and jumble in our minds. We had some idea of the finished result, but no real framework on which to hang all the project costs, work schedules and management activities. The creation of the WBS has started the planning process and has created some sort of order out of the primeval soup that was the original project concept.

Compiling the WBS has helped us identify all the principal work and cost elements. It has given us a basis for allocating major chunks of the work and deciding how many contractors and subcontractors we are going to need. We can base our cost estimate on this structure, starting from the very lowest levels of the WBS and rolling up the estimates from the bottom until we get our first attempt at an accurate cost estimate for the entire project.

Coding the WBS gives us a foundation for setting up a computer database from which many project reports can be generated when the actual work starts. Although the amounts of data will be vast, coding provides a basis for filtering and sorting the data so that each manager gets only the information that he or she needs to know, without having to be bothered or bewildered by a regular ration of enormous piles of printout.

So we have achieved much already in planning the UFO shopping mall project. Now it's time to think about putting everything into a timeframe.

The core purpose of the WBS is to systematically break down a project of mind-boggling scope into elements that each manager on the project can more easily understand and deal with.

Planning and scheduling phase 3 of the UFO shopping mall project

If one of the main reasons for creating the WBS is to make the project more understandable to each of the many managers, then it is only logical and sensible to ask the manager of each higher-level WBS element to create the detailed schedule for his or her work. You, as the overall project manager, will probably want to insist that everyone uses either the same software, or at least software that gives compatible data, so that all the information can be merged into the whole project on your main server's database. This means that you will need to exert your authority over some, if not all, of the larger contractors who are going to help build this project. You might even want to see something about specifying the planning tools and methods to be used written into their contracts.

The top-level summary plan

A very large project such as this can, surprisingly, be controlled from the top using a relatively simple summary master plan. This master plan starts the whole planning process and may contain only the tasks in the top two or three levels of the WBS. It might not even be necessary to draw a critical path network diagram; it may be enough at first to give everyone a simple bar chart, such as the one shown in Figure 5.6. This is suitable for discussion with both the senior management of this project and all the principal contractors. It can also set the provisional time framework for the entire project.

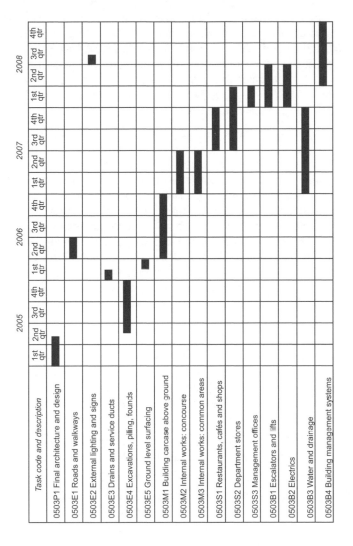

Figure 5.6 *Provisional plan for the UFO shopping mall project.*
This master sets the target times for all more detailed plans on this project

It is not feasible, practical, necessary, wise or usual to show routine administration and management activities on any schedule. For example, your work as the manager of this project is continuous, understood, unplanned (but not, we hope, unappreciated). So, not every coded item in the WBS can or needs to be planned and scheduled. I have chosen to omit from the Figure 5.6 summary plan the following level 3 items of the WBS:

0503A1: legal and general contracts

0503A2: marketing and public relations

0503A3: finance and accounting

0503A4: recruitment and employment

0503P2: project planning and control

The plan presented in Figure 5.6 takes the project to the point where shop units and larger premises for department stores can be handed over to the tenants for internal decoration and shopfitting. It might be argued, with good cause, that 0503A1 and 0503A4 should be represented on the summary plan because these are tasks that have the potential for causing project delays. For clarity, the planning periods are marked as annual quarters, whereas calendar months would be more appropriate in practice.

The manager or contractor for every task shown on the summary plan must try to schedule his or her portion of the project in detail, certainly now using critical path methods, to demonstrate how he or she will be able to meet the target dates dictated by the master plan. During this process it is probable that some of the managers and contractors will find it impossible to plan between the targets they have been given, and they will then have to negotiate some extension to the time allowed. This in turn will mean reviewing the original master plan. Although, of course, every effort will have to be made to plan for the earliest possible finish, there is no point in setting out with a plan that some know will be impossible to achieve, and which does not have the support and commitment of all the managers and contractors in the project.

Each manager and each contractor should only accept a schedule that is feasible and to which they can honestly agree to be committed.

Thus, once we have our WBS and summary plan, our shopping mall project planning will need at least one planning meeting involving all the principal players, and we must be prepared to revise the summary plan during this process to arrive at a schedule that can realistically be achieved and is accepted by all those responsible for doing the work.

We must not forget the possible risks facing this project, and this bullet must be bitten now, at the beginning. Risk management is dealt with in Chapter 8.

Before leaving this subject of the master or summary plan, please have a look at the example in Figure 5.6 and note how this plan has been presented. The timescale is made clear. Everything is laid out clearly. Each task has its description written on the chart, along with its WBS code. My reason for emphasizing these points stems from common mistakes that I see in the work of students. The two mistakes that I see most often are as follows:

- A perfectly good coded WBS is developed for the project, but then the codes are ignored in subsequent plans and reports or even replaced by different ID numbers and codes in bar charts, networks and cost estimates.
- A neat bar chart or network diagram is drawn that sets out all the tasks in their logical sequence but fails to label each task with its description, so that the chart tells its reader nothing about what each bar means.

Even the most well calculated schedule means nothing if it is not presented to the user with all the information clearly shown. Every plan must communicate.

Detailed hierarchical plans for phase 3 of the UFO shopping mall project

The complete set of plans for any complex project will comprise the master summary plan which breaks down into a series of more detailed plans, each of which corresponds to one of the elements in the upper levels of the WBS. It is highly preferable that all these plans are compiled using the same precedence network method and that they should be processed by software that can write the data to the common project management server.

The project manager must therefore arrange for the master summary plan, if it did not start out as a network, to be redrawn as a precedence network diagram. Each manager of an element from the WBS must then produce a detailed network diagram covering the work involved in completing that element. The project manager will need to ensure that the master network contains at least one task that corresponds with the start and finish of the associated more detailed network. The computer will be able to make all the necessary links between the master network and its satellites if common interface tasks are strategically placed. An interface task is really a task that occurs in two different networks, which the computer will recognize by their common task ID as being an interface.

The design of networks and the identification and treatment of common interfaces is best done by a person with considerable planning experience. There is more than one way of solving the problem but, if you are a complete beginner, you will need to seek expert help at this stage. Your software supplier may be able to help.

Figure 5.7 (see page 66) shows the conversion of the bar chart in Figure 5.6 to a master precedence diagram for the UFO shopping mall project. The small space available here means that this is more cramped than usual and the logic is not quite correct. For example, some of the complex constraints described in Chapter 3 would probably be needed here in practice. However, this summary network is perfectly adequate for demonstrating the principle.

Every task on this chart is a summary of work to be done by one or more contractors. Each of those subcontractors will be expected to develop a detailed network diagram covering their part of the project, together with a working schedule that will allow the achievement of the dates derived from time analysis of the project master network.

Some of the abbreviations in this network are severe. That is fairly usual in network diagrams, where space within the task boxes is often limited. Showing full descriptions would mean drawing or plotting the network on an enormous roll of paper. Sometimes the relevant computer fields also restrict the number of characters that can be entered, again leading to the need for savage abbreviations.

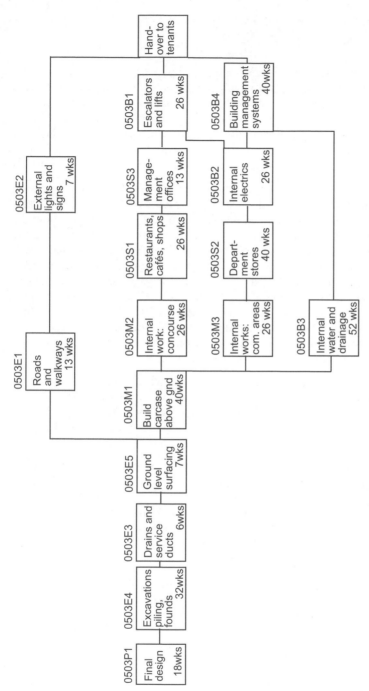

Figure 5.7 *Master network for the UFO shopping mall project.*
Each task breaks down into a more detailed network at a lower WBS level

Putting things into perspective

Being responsible for planning a project as large as the UFO shopping mall requires considerable training, experience and aptitude. These qualities are far beyond those possessed by the average beginner and are acquired only by a few people and then only after some years in the profession. However, this shopping mall project will employ a great many different contractors. Many of those individual contractors will have their own project managers, who must plan and control the work of their own companies. So here we have a project where the top project manager needs to be something approaching a genius, but in which a far greater number of project managers need only be competent in techniques that are far more straightforward and easy to learn.

If all projects were the size of the shopping mall, therefore, perhaps only 1 per cent of all the project managers in our nation would need to be expert in the development of work breakdowns and hierarchical network diagrams on this scale. But, of course, there are many hundreds of far smaller projects, especially in the construction industry, that are nowhere near as big as the shopping mall and they can be planned adequately with far less sophisticated methods.

This means that there might be thousands of people who need project management skills, but only a tiny fraction of those people will be at the head of very large projects at the genius level. Most of us will be quite competent provided that we have enough common sense and the ability to put jobs in their practical sequence in a plan. Take heart, therefore, if you are a beginner. The chances are that you will be able to manage your project successfully if you can draw a simple network diagram and apply a fair amount of common sense when using the results at the workplace. If you have access to a computer, and know how to use it, so much the better, because that can remove much of the drudgery and make your plans far more flexible. The next chapter takes an introductory look at the use of popular project management software for scheduling small projects.

Chapter **6**

Getting Help from the Computer

Computers came to the aid of project managers in the late 1960s, since when no respectable project manager has really been able to contemplate planning and controlling a project without one. Even the very early mainframe machines, with their punched card data input and memories measured in kilobytes, could perform many of the operations that are possible today. But they took a little longer to do their work, had to be coaxed by experts in white coats and air-conditioned dust-free rooms, and the machines were incredibly expensive. Enormous reports came from a line printer with practically no graphics capabilities and you could have any colour you wanted as long as it was somewhere between black and faint grey, depending on the age of the printer ribbon.

Now, of course, everyone has access to cheap computing power that eclipses the slow speed and inconvenience of those early systems. We are no longer kept waiting for data sheets or punched cards to go for batch processing, to be returned to us a week later.

The Internet has revolutionized communications, which is a tremendous advantage in our industry, with its particular problems of work sites that can be great distances from the home office. Mining companies used to send prospectors out into the wilderness with a donkey or two to keep them company and carry their gear, and nothing would be seen or heard of men or donkeys for months. Now satellite communications keep us in touch and we can swap drawings and photographs with sites in the remotest of places.

Also very important is the wealth of choice in software today, which contrasts well with the very early days when some of the very few programs available, though advertised as 'powerful', were simply not up to the job at all. We have to read all advertisements with a degree of scepticism but, with project management software at least, it can be said that we've never had it so good. The construction industry has a proud record in this field; it has never been slow to exploit this technology and, from the very early days, it has been responsible for some ingenious innovations.

A software advertisement once declared 'If you can move a mouse you can manage your project!' People really do get some very silly ideas!

Overheard comment: 'It must be good because the advertisements speak so highly of it.'

Capabilities of project management software

Although there are programs that use linked bar charts as the basis for their scheduling, by far the best practice is always to draw a network diagram for the project before going to the computer. It will have to be a precedence network diagram (PDM) because the other kind of network (arrow diagrams or ADM) cannot be processed by any modern software. For that reason alone, arrow network diagrams are not described in this book. The remainder of this chapter, therefore, assumes that every project that we manage will be planned from the start with a precedence network diagram if it is going to be scheduled by computer.

Arrow network diagrams, which are easier to sketch than precedence network diagrams, are described in all editions of Project Management, written by Dennis Lock and published by Gower.

Data error checks

Remember GIGO: garbage in – garbage out.

Although computers have a reputation for being mechanistic machines that will plough blindly on when we mere humans feed them with wrong information, most project management software will carry out diagnostic checks on our project data. The computer will either warn that the data being entered appear to be wrong or it will report our mistakes when it tries to do the calculations. Dangles and loops are certain to be detected and reported. So the computer can prevent us from making some silly mistakes. But the machine cannot read our minds and if we enter the duration of a task as 100 days when we intended 10 days, then our schedules will show that task as lasting for 100 days and the mistake can only be put right when someone spots it. Let's hope that we find all such mistakes before our clients do.

Time analysis

One nanosecond is 10^{-9} seconds, which in layman's language is one thousand millionth of a second.

Most project management software performs time analysis for medium-sized networks in nanoseconds. Programs such as Microsoft Project carry out time analysis continuously and update the results as soon as each new task is entered. On some other programs, 'Tools' must be selected from the toolbar, and time analysis is then selected from the drop-down menu.

We can be certain that, if our input data are correct, there will be no mistakes in the time analysis results. Better still, we can forget the simple day or week numbers that we had to use on hand-drawn networks because the computer will calculate all our project schedules using calendar dates.

Resources and costs

The computer can schedule resources and calculate project costs. The results can be plotted as resource histograms, time/cost graphs or as spreadsheets. Spreadsheets can include cash outflow forecasts. When we have eventually become sufficiently clever in drawing the project network with enough detail, the resource scheduling capability can even be used to forecast a net cash flow schedule.

Filtering and sorting

Filtering selects what goes into a report and sorting puts the filtered items into the sequence that you want.

The computer can be instructed to produce reports that sort all the tasks into some convenient sequence, such as their earliest start dates. If tasks are given codes relating to the managers or departments that are going to be responsible for doing the work, then the reports can be filtered, so that each manager or department gets reports covering only those tasks containing their own particular code.

Changing or updating the schedule

A great characteristic of computer-generated schedules is that they can easily be changed to take account of progress or changes to the project. Changing any chart produced by manual methods can be extremely tedious, but the computer makes such changes almost too easy.

When a change is made, or as progress information is entered and the plans are updated, the computer can sometimes store the original schedule as a baseline, so that changes from our original intentions can be seen by comparing the new schedule and actual results against the baseline. However, I must confess that I have never used this feature myself, because I don't like looking back and prefer always to think about what we must be doing next.

The workshop project meets the computer

The workshop project that provided examples for Chapters 2 and 3 can be used here to show a few capabilities of project management software. The task list is given in Table 6.1. This is based on the task list for this project that first appeared as Table 2.1 in Chapter 2 (see p. 13). I have updated a few of the descriptions and cost estimates but this new task is essentially unchanged from the earlier version and still agrees with the network diagram in Chapter 3 (see Figure 3.7, pp. 34–5).

Task ID	Task description	Duration (days)	Resources L	Resources S	Material costs (£)	Prede-cessors
01	Clear site and mark out	1	1	1	0	–
02	Dig soakaway and trench	1	1		0	01
03	Base formwork	1		1	40	01
04	Position underground pipes	1	1	1	60	02
05	Pour base concrete	1	1		80	03
06	Pour hard standing for cars	1	1		70	04
07	Cure base concrete	5				05
08	Position door frame	1	1	1	100	07
09	Brick walls to eaves	5	1	1	750	08
10	Fit RSJ lintel	1	1	1	30	09
11	Fit window frame	1	1	1	75	09
12	Hang doors	1	1	1	25	10
13	Finish brickwork	2	1	1	30	10, 11
14	Prime doors and window	1		1	20	12
15	Cut and fit roof timbers	3	1	1	180	13
16	Glaze windows	1		1	30	14
17	Paint doors	1		1	20	14
18	Cap parapets	1	1	1	40	15
19	Fit roof sheets	2	1	1	200	15
20	Paint window frame	1		1	10	16
21	Fit door furniture	1		1	35	17
22	Fit gutters and downpipes	1	1	1	60	04, 18
23	Seal roof	1		1	70	19
24	Install electrics	2		1	160	19
25	Clear away site and skips	1	1		120	06, 20, 21, 22, 23, 24.

Table 6.1 *Revised task list for the workshop project*

Material costs for the workshop project

There are several ways of scheduling materials costs in the computer. They can be treated like a normal re-usable resource in the same way as people, so that, for example, the £750 needed for the five days of task 09 could be specified as a cost resource to be spent at the rate of £150 per day. Another option, which is also allowed by most computer software, is simply to specify that task 09 will cost £750. You will need to check how your own particular chosen software deals with costs and whether specifying a cost for the task will interfere with the calculated costs for the resources used on the task.

The materials costs shown in Table 6.1 do not include the hiring costs of any machinery used. We could have scheduled the use of hire plant by naming each item of machinery as a resource and specifying the requirements on each task. But there would be no point in doing this for this tiny project because we only have two people on site and they do not expect to need to use more than one piece of hire plant at the same time. So common sense and a look at the final schedules will tell these worthy workers when to hire their plant. But on a larger project, there *would* be a case for scheduling each item of hire plant, just like any other re-usable resource.

Network links

It is not always necessary to draw a task list. Experienced planners can read the data into the computer directly from the network diagram.

The final column in Table 6.1 lists, for each task, the ID codes of the tasks that immediately precede it in the network diagram. Entering these ID codes into the computer is one way of inserting the network links. Obviously there can be no predecessor entry for the task that comes right at the beginning. Entering the predecessor task ID codes effectively defines the network pattern (we call it the network logic) for the computer, enabling it to make the correct forward and backward passes through the network. Specifying an incorrect link or forgetting to put one in can create loops and dangles.

Dates and calendars

If the computer is given no information on project working hours, it will probably use a default calendar contained within the software, which is based on working from Monday to Friday each week. The computer will probably assume a working weekday of eight hours. However, although some programs can mix days, hours and even minutes in the same schedule, it is far better to use just one kind of time, such as hours, days or weeks. I usually prefer to use days.

Unless told otherwise, the computer software will assign each task in the workshop project to the default calendar. However, the planner has the option to modify the default calendar or introduce different calendars that would apply to tasks on different parts of the project. So we might have the default calendar applying to tasks at a British headquarters, with a completely different calendar allocated to tasks that are to be carried out in the Middle East. That would take account of different holidays and work patterns in the two countries.

A mix of different shift working times in the same project could also be taken care of using a different calendar for each pattern of working times. Tasks to be done during normal hours would be assigned (automatically) to the default calendar, and the jobs to be done over two or three shifts could be attached to the special calendar.

Time analysis of the workshop project using Microsoft Project 2000

Microsoft Project is by far the most popular project management software in terms of sales and the number of users. Very early versions had some flaws but this package is being developed continuously and the most serious malfunctions disappeared with the introduction of Microsoft Project 98. Processing for this part of the chapter was done using Microsoft Project 2000, and later versions are available that have even more capability.

Data entry

Microsoft Project 2000 is very user-friendly, especially for all who are familiar with the usual functions of Microsoft Windows and Microsoft Office applications. It took only a few minutes to enter the workshop project data and produce the time analysis report shown later for the workshop project in Figure 6.1 (p. 76). I gave a similar project to a group of students as an exercise. Most had never even seen Microsoft Project before, but each of them, with very little coaching, had the time analysis and a cost report ready in about 15 minutes.

When the program is opened, a blank bar chart screen appears. The left-hand side of this 'Gantt chart' view has a few columns into which data can be entered directly. So the description for the first task can immediately be typed in by selecting the top space in the 'name' column. When you enter this name for the first task you will notice that the task ID code 1 is automatically assigned and you are prompted to enter the name for the next task, which will automatically be given 2 as its ID code.

As you enter the name for each task, it is automatically given a duration estimate of one day and a bar appears in the chart section of the screen on the right-hand area of the screen. When you have entered all the task names, you have created a task record in the computer database for each of the 25 tasks in this workshop project.

The bar chart view is always called the 'Gantt chart' view in Microsoft Project.

The next step is to check each task duration against the network diagram or the task list (Table 6.1) and, where necessary, change the default duration of one day to the correct duration. Now the screen on the right-hand side will show all the bars at their correct timescale lengths, but they will all be shown starting from today's date.

Now you need to enter the network links, so that the computer 'sees' the project network pattern. There are at least three ways in which this can be done, but I suggest that you select the column headed predecessor and, for each task, type in the ID codes of its immediately preceding tasks. You can find these ID codes by examining the network diagram or you can simply look at the task list in Table 6.1. As you enter each link, you should notice that the bars in the right-hand section of the screen start jumping along to their correct positions.

Selecting 'project' from the toolbar allows project information to be entered, the most important piece of information here being the start date of the project. Type in the date that you want and check that this date then appears as the start of the first task in the Gantt chart view.

Customized reports for the workshop project after time analysis

Microsoft Project 2000 allows a great deal of customization. Go to the 'view' toolbar to select either the Gantt chart or the network screen. Customization 'wizards' are available in both the Gantt chart and network views simply by selecting 'layout' from the menu in the 'format' toolbar. The various functions will soon be discovered with very little trial and error.

Microsoft Project uses the American preference of 'slack' instead of 'float'. Don't worry – the two words mean the same thing.

In the Gantt chart view it is possible to insert or hide columns in the table on the left-hand section of the screen. All insertions can be picked from a browser that drops down in the insertion window. You can make more room for the columns by dragging the vertical dividing line between the table and the chart to the right using the mouse.

If a row of hatching appears in any box instead of the text that you expect, it means that the column is too narrow to accommodate all the text. So you will need to widen the column, which is easily done in Microsoft Project by clicking on the right-hand vertical rule of the column and dragging it a little to the right.

The customized version of the workshop project time analysis table shown in Figure 6.1 was produced using the methods just described. You might like to compare the results with the equivalent manually produced table shown in Table 3.1 (p. 37). Although we now have calendar dates instead of day numbers, you will notice that the free float and total float results agree.

ID	Task name	Duration	Early start	Early finish	Late start	Late finish	Free slack	Total slack
1	Clear site and mark out	1 day?	06 Jun '05	06 Jun '05	06 Jun '05	06 Jun '05	0 days?	0 days?
2	Dig soakaway and trench	1 day?	07 Jun '05	07 Jun '05	05 Jul '05	05 Jul '05	0 days?	20 days?
3	Make formwork for base	1 day?	07 Jun '05	07 Jun '05	07 Jun '05	07 Jun '05	0 days?	0 days?
4	Position u/g pipes	1 day?	08 Jun '05	08 Jun '05	06 Jul '05	06 Jul '05	0 days?	20 days?
5	Pour base concrete	1 day?	08 Jun '05	08 Jun '05	08 Jun '05	08 Jun '05	0 days?	0 days?
6	Pour hard standing for cars	1 day?	09 Jun '05	09 Jun '05	07 Jul '05	07 Jul '05	20 days?	20 days?
7	Cure base concrete	5 days?	09 Jun '05	15 Jun '05	09 Jun '05	15 Jun '05	0 days?	0 days?
8	Position door frame	1 day?	16 Jun '05	16 Jun '05	16 Jun '05	16 Jun '05	0 days?	0 days?
9	Brick walls to eaves	5 days?	17 Jun '05	23 Jun '05	17 Jun '05	23 Jun '05	0 days?	0 days?
10	Fit RSJ lintel	1 day?	24 Jun '05	24 Jun '05	24 Jun '05	24 Jun '05	0 days?	0 days?
11	Fit window frame	1 day?	24 Jun '05	24 Jun '05	04 Jul '05	04 Jul '05	0 days?	5 days?
12	Hang doors	1 day?	27 Jun '05	27 Jun '05	27 Jun '05	28 Jun '05	0 days?	0 days?
13	Finish brickwork	2 days?	27 Jun '05	28 Jun '05	05 Jul '05	05 Jul '05	0 days?	5 days?
14	Prime doors and window	1 day?	28 Jun '05	28 Jun '05	29 Jun '05	01 Jul '05	0 days?	5 days?
15	Cut and fit roof timbers	3 days?	29 Jun '05	01 Jul '05	29 Jun '05	06 Jul '05	0 days?	0 days?
16	Glaze windows	1 day?	29 Jun '05	29 Jun '05	06 Jul '05	06 Jul '05	0 days?	5 days?
17	Paint doors	1 day?	29 Jun '05	29 Jun '05	06 Jul '05	06 Jul '05	0 days?	5 days?
18	Cap parapets	1 day?	04 Jul '05	04 Jul '05	06 Jul '05	06 Jul '05	0 days?	2 days?
19	Fit roof sheets	2 days?	04 Jul '05	05 Jul '05	04 Jul '05	05 Jul '05	0 days?	0 days?
20	Paint window frame	1 day?	30 Jun '05	30 Jun '05	07 Jul '05	07 Jul '05	5 days?	5 days?
21	Fit door furniture	1 day?	30 Jun '05	30 Jun '05	07 Jul '05	07 Jul '05	5 days?	5 days?
22	Fit gutters and downpipes	1 day?	05 Jul '05	05 Jul '05	07 Jul '05	07 Jul '05	2 days?	2 days?
23	Seal roof	1 day?	06 Jul '05	06 Jul '05	07 Jul '05	07 Jul '05	1 day?	1 day?
24	Install electrics	2 days?	06 Jul '05	07 Jul '05	06 Jul '05	07 Jul '05	0 days?	0 days?
25	Clear away site and skips	1 day?	08 Jul '05	08 Jul '05	08 Jul '05	08 Jul '05	0 days?	0 days?

Figure 6.1 *Workshop project time analysis by Microsoft Project 2000*

All the reports from computers in this chapter are simulations, copied faithfully from the originals using a drawing program to remove non-essential elements and improve clarity.

The bar chart shown in Figure 6.2 has been customized to remove links between the tasks because these clutter and confuse the picture. Critical tasks on the original were coloured red, and they are shown solid black in our version. When printing, it is important to specify the 'from' and 'to' dates correctly when the print window appears. If this is not done, and a project start date has been specified that is months or years ahead, the printer will happily start printing a pile of substantially blank sheets starting from today's date until it gets to the actual project, wasting heaps of time and paper.

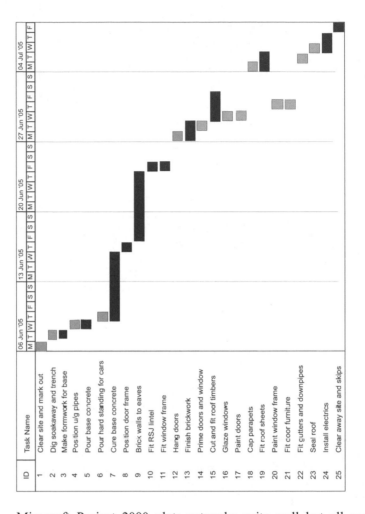

Figure 6.2 *Workshop project Gantt chart by Microsoft Project 2000. The horizontal scale has been reduced to fit this page*

Microsoft Project 2000 plots networks quite well but all project management software takes up a great deal of space on the screen and on the printed page in the process. Although the network view can be zoomed out to include all the activities, it has to be kept fairly large if all the text is to be legible. Pushing the print button even for this very simple project caused eight A4 sheets to spew from the printer. Just five of the total 25 tasks appeared on the first page, the significant contents of which are shown in Figure 6.3. This could be improved by manual manipulation of the task boxes on the screen, but that can be an extremely tedious chore.

Figure 6.4 is an enlarged detail of one of the task boxes from Figure 6.3, redrawn at a size that can be read without using a microscope. This is the default format for a task box. It is possible to customize the shape, size, colour and content of task boxes. The horizontal and vertical spacing between boxes in the network is also easy to change, and this can sometimes reduce the overall size of the plot and the amount of paper needed to print it.

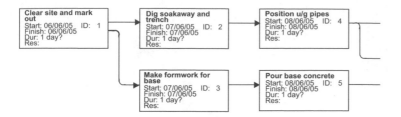

Figure 6.3 *Page 1 of the workshop project network (Microsoft Project 2000)*

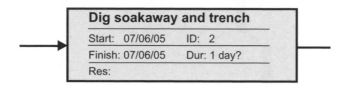

Figure 6.4 *Detail from Figure 6.3 at full-scale size*

Cash outflow report

If you have decided not to go on to the resource scheduling step, you could use the task list in Table 6.1 to calculate the cost for each task (resources plus materials) and enter the results directly into the computer. Look, for example, at task 15, which is 'Cut and fit roof timbers'. This task needs one skilled person and one labourer for three days each and £180 of materials. If the cost per day of a labourer is £80, and for a skilled person £120, the costs for this task should be as follows:

Item	£
• Labourer, 3 days at £80	240.00
• Skilled, 3 days at £120	360.00
• Materials	180.00
Total task cost	780.00

You can calculate the cost for each task in this way and enter all these costs in the cost column in the Gantt chart view. Then, go to 'View' in toolbar and select 'Reports'. Next select 'Costs' and finally click on the large 'Cash flow' icon. Figure 6.5 shows the cash outflow schedule for the workshop project, as calculated by Microsoft Project 2000, using this method. This is a very useful standard report available automatically from the program, and in this case it shows that the workshop is expected to cost a total of £7605.00 (excluding hire plant).

	06/06/05	13/06/05	20/06/05	27/06/05	04/07/05	Total
Clear site and mark out	£200.00					£200.00
Dig soakaway and trench	£80.00					£80.00
Make formwork for base	£160.00					£160.00
Position u/g pipes	£260.00					£260.00
Pour base concrete	£160.00					£160.00
Pour hard standing for cars	£150.00					£150.00
Cure base concrete						
Position door frame		£300.00				£300.00
Brick walls to eaves		£350.00	£1400.00			£1750.00
Fit RSJ lintel			£230.00			£230.00
Fit window frame			£275.00			£275.00
Hang doors				£225.00		£225.00
Finish brickwork				£430.00		£430.00
Prime doors and windows				£140.00		£140.00
Cut and fit roof timbers				£780.00		£780.00
Glaze windows				£150.00		£150.00
Paint doors				£140.00		£140.00
Cap parapets					£240.00	£240.00
Fit roof sheets					£600.00	£600.00
Paint window frame				£130.00		£130.00
Fit door furniture				£155.00		£155.00
Fit gutters and downpipes					£260.00	£260.00
Seal roof					£190.00	£190.00
Install electrics					£400.00	£400.00
Clear away site and skips					£200.00	£200.00
Total	**£1010.00**	**£650.00**	**£1905.00**	**£2150.00**	**£1890.00**	**£7605.00**

Figure 6.5 *Workshop project cash outflow estimate produced by Microsoft Project 2000 before resource scheduling*

Resource scheduling of the workshop project by Primavera SureTrak Project Manager

Microsoft Project 2000 can lead the beginner into some traps when carrying out resource scheduling, the most serious of which causes your carefully chosen task durations to be changed, sometimes into decimal quantities. This is because the program, in its default state, considers each task to be a piece of work containing a constant number of work hours rather than having a chosen duration. So the program can, during resource scheduling, change the amount of resources assigned to a task and change the duration of the task accordingly.

However, I used the program to produce the data from which the histograms in Figure 6.6 were drawn. There were some small errors in the reported results (especially in the cost totals) that I had to check and correct manually.

The numbers shown in the resources column of Table 6.1 relate to the 'workforce' of the very small company that is going to build this workshop. This is a father and son business, with the son at present regarded as a labourer (L) and the father as a skilled person (S) with good all-round capabilities. The father can switch happily between bricklaying, plastering, roofing, plumbing and electrical wiring without making too many serious mistakes. The son has strong muscles, and we hope that the rest will come later.

There are many instances, even in large projects, where some resources do not need to be scheduled. If the most highly used resources are scheduled, that should produce a smooth work pattern

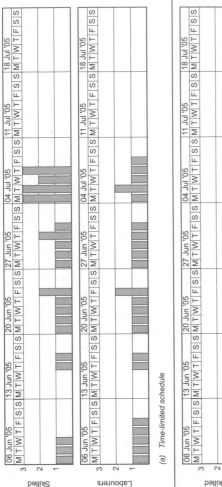
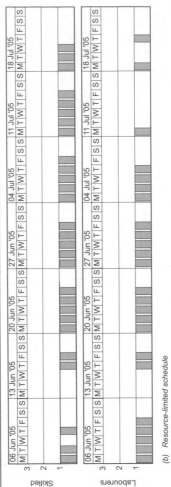

(a) Time-limited schedule

(b) Resource-limited schedule

Figure 6.6 Workshop project resource usage patterns using data from Microsoft Project 2000

If you should decide to schedule resources, start by keeping things simple and schedule only those resources that usually get overloaded.

generally and we usually find that this also smoothes out the use of all the other resources, whether they have been scheduled or not. Decisions on which resources to schedule will be made based on experience. However, it is obvious that both the skilled person and the labourer are key resources in this workshop project, so both have been scheduled.

When this project is entered in the computer it will be necessary to define each class of resource, giving the code (L or S in this case), the resource name, the dates between which the resource can be made available, the cost per day for each person and the number (amount) of each type of resource available for the project on each working day.

The numeral 1 in each of the L and S columns in Table 6.1 means that one person of that resource type will be needed for the relevant task. It can be seen that some tasks need one skilled person, others one labourer and yet others need both one labourer and one skilled person working together. In every case for this project it is assumed that the resources will be needed at constant rate from the beginning to the end of each task. So, for instance, five days for 1S and 1L means that you expect one skilled person and one labourer to work on the task full-time for five days.

In this simple project, with only one person of each category available, it is clear that the resource availability must be given as 1S and 1L. Some programs allow the user to specify a higher 'threshold' number as being available, for the computer to use if the project cannot be finished on time within the normal resource limits. Overtime or casual labour can sometimes be used as threshold resources to offset a few overloads, but overtime should be held back as a reserve and should not normally be scheduled at all. Threshold resources can be given a higher daily cost rate to allow for the fact that overtime or casual labour rates might be higher.

The cost per day of the skilled person will be assumed as £120 per eight-hour day, and as £80 for the labourer. These rates are for the small family business with no overheads. They would, of course, be higher for a larger company with more infrastructure to support.

Data entered for this part of the scheduling process were as follows:

L = labourer costs £80 per day per person
S = skilled costs £120 per day per person
M = materials costs, as shown in the task list of Table 6.1.
The availability of each resource L and S was given as one of each (entered in Microsoft Project 2000 as 100 per cent of each).

The schedules were run in both time-limited and resource-limited modes. Data from these schedules were first checked for errors and then used to produce the charts shown in Figure 6.6.

Notice that, in the time-limited schedule at the top of Figure 6.6, Microsoft Project 2000 correctly found it necessary to exceed the numbers of resources available if the project is to be finished by its earliest possible date of 8 July 2005. This problem was particularly acute for the skilled workers, with three being needed on some days when only one will be available.

When the computer was instructed not to exceed the resource levels available, this resulted (as expected) in the timescale for the project being extended. So, as the charts in the lower half of Figure 6.6 show, the project end date has been extended by two weeks to 21 July 2005. Tabular reports corresponding to each of these resource schedules were available from the Gantt chart view.

I used Primavera SureTrak Project Planner (version 3) to run these resource schedules again. The results differed slightly from those produced by Microsoft Project 2000, the most significant difference being that the completion date for the workshop project is shown one day later, at 22 July 2005. But this software did not make the small errors seen in the Microsoft Project 2000 output. The table in Figure 6.7 is the work-to list produced by Primavera SureTrak Project Manager, showing just the relevant columns. These are the dates which, if kept to, will ensure that on no day will the resources needed exceed those that you have stated to be available. In this case, it means that no day needs more than one skilled person and one labourer.

Dates in work-to lists produced after this kind of resource scheduling are sometimes called scheduled dates. They should lie somewhere between the earliest and latest dates indicated by network time analysis and are the dates that should be followed to obtain the smoothest and most efficient use of the project resources.

Act ID	Description	Original duration	Early start	Early finish
Workshop				
10	Clear site and mark out	1	06JUN05	06JUN05
30	Make formwork for base	1	07JUN05	07JUN05
20	Dig soakaway and trench	1	08JUN05	08JUN05
50	Pour base concrete	1	08JUN05	08JUN05
40	Position u/g pipes	1	09JUN05	09JUN05
70	Cure base concrete	5	09JUN05	15JUN05
60	Pour hard standing for cars	1	10JUN05	10JUN05
80	Position door frame	1	16JUN05	16JUN05
90	Brick walls to eaves	5	17JUN05	23JUN05
100	Fit RSJ lintel	1	24JUN05	24JUN05
110	Fit window frame	1	27JUN05	27JUN05
130	Finish brickwork	2	28JUN05	29JUN05
150	Cut and fit roof timbers	3	30JUN05	05JUL05
190	Fit roof sheets	2	06JUL05	06JUL05
180	Cap parapets	1	08JUL05	08JUL05
240	Install electrics	2	08JUL05	11JUL05
120	Hang doors	1	11JUL05	11JUL05
220	Fit gutters and downpipes	1	12JUL05	12JUL05
230	Seal roof	1	12JUL05	12JUL05
140	Prime doors and windows	1	15JUL05	15JUL05
160	Glaze windows	1	18JUL05	18JUL05
170	Paint doors	1	19JUL05	19JUL05
200	Paint window frame	1	20JUL05	20JUL05
210	Fit door furniture	1	21JUL05	21JUL05
250	Clear away site and skips	1	22JUL05	22JUL05

Figure 6.7 *Work-to list (Primavera SureTrak Project Manager)*

Choosing project management software

There is a vast, even bewildering, array of software available. All suppliers claim great things for their products, and some of those claims might be justified. Software can be classified roughly by price. So there is a cheap end of the market, a mid-price and a high-end. Programs at the cheap end will have very limited functionality and are little more than simple charting programs.

Foremost in the middle range is Microsoft Project, and this makes a very good choice, at least for the serious beginner, in its Microsoft Project 2000 and later versions. Some training will be needed, especially if costs and resources are to be scheduled without errors.

High-end systems will need more cash investment and some serious training. But, if your projects are fairly big and you are trying to manage several at the same time, this training and investment will soon be repaid in increased efficiency, fewer missed deadlines and reduced overall project costs. Primavera is a high-end program that has long been especially popular with the construction industry and is relatively easy to use. Artemis has a good reputation, at the top of the high-end price range. Open Plan is not user-friendly at first, but has been developed sensitively over many years and is liked by many professional planners (including me). Lesser known, but with the most adaptability and functionality of all, is the software from 4c Systems.

Buying and installing new software means investing not only in the actual purchase price, but also in the hours of training needed and in the time to enter all the data for your projects and processing the data. If you have made the wrong choice, you, and those who work for you, are likely to be put off computers for life. So it pays to make the best choice in the first place. More advice on choosing project management software can be found in all the more recent editions of my larger book, *Project Management*, published by Gower.

Further explanation of the methods for using this and other programs in resource scheduling will not be given here, because hands-on training is really required to learn the techniques. However, the effort, once made, will be found most worthwhile if head office resources or directly employed labour have to be scheduled for medium- to large-sized projects.

Chapter **7**

Organizing the Larger Project

Construction project organization is a particularly complex subject, not least because of the way in which the organization depends on the size of the project and the nature of the contract. One peculiarity is that the organization does not stay put in one place, but changes fairly early on in the project so that the main action moves from the home office to a site that might be many miles away. So our organizations range from cases where (as in the workshop project) there is no obvious project organization at all to large projects where there are both large home office and site organizations. So this chapter cannot describe a typical construction project organization because there is no such thing as 'typical' in our industry. What we can do, however, is illustrate some of the principles that apply to organizations in general and show how these relate to the home office. Then we can take a brief look at the elements that might be found in a large site organization.

Charting the organization

Although there is no perfect method, a chart can be drawn to depict any business organization. Figure 7.1 shows the usual convention for drawing such charts (which some misguided people call 'organigrams'). The reason that charts are not perfect is that they cannot show all the intricate details of how people behave and react with each other in real life. They can only show the intentions of the person or people who designed the organization.

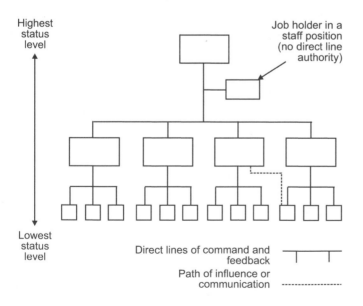

The recommended convention is to put job titles, not people's names in the boxes. The argument is that people come and go but the organization is relatively stable. But such rules are made to be broken.

Figure 7.1 *How to interpret an organization chart*

The arrangement of Figure 7.1 shows a line and function organization. It has a well defined line structure, so that commands can be issued from the top, down through the lines, to the various departmental managers, and they in turn can issue commands to juniors further down. Each departmental manager is responsible for a specialist function of the business, such as building design, services design, financial management, purchasing, marketing and so on. So these departmental managers are sometimes called functional managers.

A person in a staff position is, to a large extent, outside the line structure. He or she has no authority to issue orders through the line, but is in a supporting or advisory position. So people like company lawyers, top secretaries, planners and the like are often found in staff positions. They have no power, but they might enjoy some status and, through their professionalism, some authority. A company lawyer might not be able to issue commands but can offer advice that others in the company would be foolish to ignore.

A manager who is held accountable for a task must be given the corresponding degree of power and authority to see the task through.

Managers issuing commands down the lines are exercising their power and authority. Those at the receiving end are held accountable for carrying out the commands handed down from above. So, a manager some way down the chart is accountable for carrying out the tasks assigned to him or her, but must be given the corresponding power and authority needed to hand down the instructions further to juniors, so that the work gets done or actions are taken.

The lines are two-way, so not only are commands passed down through them, but also feedback is passed back up the lines to tell the more senior managers of successes, failures or problems needing their attention or supporting action.

Some companies try to avoid the problem of perceived status by drawing their organization charts with all the names arranged around a circle. This is the 'round-table' principle, but it still doesn't work too well because even round charts have a top and a bottom.

All this might seem fairly straightforward but problems can arise even from the moment when we try to draw the organization chart. One problem is that people often have differing, sometimes elevated, ideas about their own status and importance. They become disappointed or angry when an organization chart is produced that shows them at a lower status level than they expect or, even worse, leaves them out of the chart altogether. Consequently in many companies, organization charts carry a little placatory note that says something like 'levels on this chart do not necessarily indicate status'. But no one really ever believes that.

Organization charts are useful in many ways. A summary chart can be given to all the key managers in the project organization, to external agencies and subcontractors, perhaps to the media, and not least to the client. Organization charts, along with a responsibility matrix (see Figure 7.9 later in this chapter) help define the responsibilities of key people in the project.

Few project managers are allowed the luxury of setting up their own project organizations. More usually they are put in an organization that has been predetermined for them by higher management or company custom. However, it pays to know a little about the principles of organization design, because the nature of the organization can have a great influence on the way in which people work together and on the ultimate success (or failure) of the project.

A manager's span of control

In a small project, employing only a handful of people, the project manager can manage all the people directly with no formal organization structure. However, most projects require more than a handful of people, and there are practical limits to the number of people that any manager should be asked to supervise directly. One manager can probably control quite a large group or gang of unskilled people, but should not be expected to control directly more than about five junior managers or supervisors. This all has to do with something known as the manager's span of control and is sometimes called the 'rule of five'. Today, this rule is not regarded as rigid and the numbers will depend on circumstances, but in most cases it would be very unwise to expect a manager to have as many as (say) ten direct subordinates.

V.A. Graicunas wrote a paper called 'The Manager's Span of Control', published in The Bulletin of the International Management Institute, March 1933, proving that no manager could adequately control more than six direct subordinate managers and recommending a maximum span of five.

Before leaving this topic, think about two different companies, each doing similar work, and each employing about the same number of people. In company A no manager has more than about three people directly responsible to him or her. In company B each manager controls ten other managers directly. So it is obvious that company B needs fewer managers than company A. Also, if we were to draw the organization charts for these two companies, company A would have more management levels in the chart than company B, making the chart for company A tall and the chart for company B relatively wide and flat.

So we talk about tall and flat organizations. A tall organization, with each manager controlling only a few other managers, means that every manager can give more attention to subordinates and to the work detail. But the people working in all the various groups under all these managers tend to be separated from each other by the vertical line structure. In other words, horizontal communication between people in different groups is made more difficult in a tall organization, and must be better in a flat organization.

In the flat organization, some managers might have so many subordinates that they cannot give each individual enough attention. So there has to be a balance between these two tall and flat extremes, which is where the rule of five can sometimes help in organization design.

Project teams and task forces

A project team or task force is the simplest kind of project organization that we can have. The principle is shown in Figure 7.2 which, you will note, follows the simple line and function structure pattern shown in Figure 7.1.

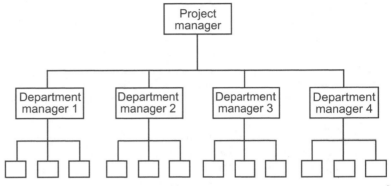

Figure 7.2 *Principle of a project team*

In a project team, the line of command to everyone working on the project comes down directly from the project manager. The line might pass through other managers, but the project manager is at the top of the project organization, in complete charge. This kind of organization has significant advantages and disadvantages.

Advantages and disadvantages of a project team or task force

If you set up a dedicated team to design and build a project, everyone working in that organization will be working on the same project, with no other work to distract them. It should be easy to develop a team spirit and encourage everyone to climb on board the roller coaster towards the eventual success of the project.

If any of the work is confidential, or even secret, keeping everything within a team helps prevent information leakages. Costing is easier, because everything spent by the organization is spent on the single project. Communication is relatively easy, and it is sometimes possible to put at least the senior people in the home office organization either in the same room or very near to each other.

The project manager at the top of the team has no conflict of power and authority with any other manager in the same company. He or she is in command, take it or leave it, and everyone knows exactly where they stand.

It's far easier to create team spirit when a team actually exists.

This is all fine when the project is in full swing, but there are difficulties when the project approaches its finish. When the excitement of the topping out ceremony is over, people start to see the end of the project as the end of their present employment. They might begin to ask, 'What shall I be doing next month, when this project finally ends?'

Another disadvantage with a team is that it can be inefficient in using the time of specialists. Suppose a company employs only one or two experts on structural steel design, but has five different project teams. It would be inefficient to take on three more experts – one for each team – because, at times, some or all of those specialists would have nothing to do. To overcome that problem we need more flexible organization that allows people to spend their time on two or more projects in the same week, or even on the same day.

Of course, when we get to the project site the organization has to be a team, because everyone works at the site and the site manager is in charge. So these questions about looking for alternatives to project team organizations really only apply to the home office organizations of fairly large construction companies and equipment manufacturers.

Figure 7.3 shows a project team organization for a fairly large company that might be working on mining or petrochemical plant construction. Note that some textbooks make a mistake here when they show administrative functions in the company – such as marketing, purchasing and accounts – as part of the project team. Although a large project team might have its own purchasing staff and a project accountant, most large organizations keep these administrative functions outside the project management organization and have them reporting to the company's general management. The only likely exception to this rule would be a company set up to build just one project, in which case everyone in the company must be part of that project team.

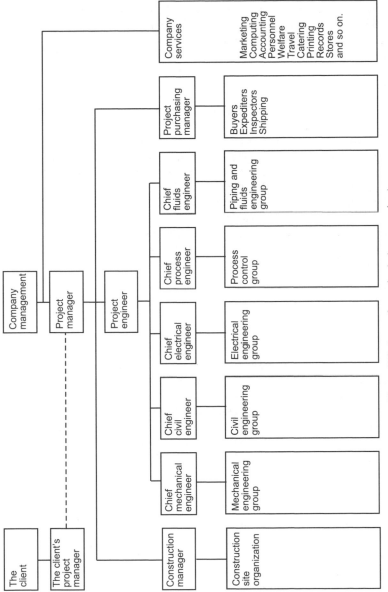

Figure 7.3 *Team for a single large project*

A project task force is similar to a team, with everyone working for one task force manager, but the implication here is that the task force has been set up specially to deal with something particularly urgent, or even to solve a crisis. The need for a task force can arise when something really serious happens on site, such as a building collapse, a mine accident or a natural disaster like an earthquake or hurricane. A task force is sometimes assembled when a project is running very late and must be pulled back on track to satisfy a purple-faced client who is jumping up and down with rage and threatening to sue everyone in sight.

So, project teams are essential on construction sites and are probably the best option at the home office for big projects lasting for many years or for shorter-term projects that are exceptionally urgent. Thus we might have a project team at the site but a completely different kind of organization structure back at the home office. You will notice that the team organization shown in Figure 7.3 includes a remote construction site team. A large company with this kind of home office organization might have a separate team for each of its big projects, with every team having its own project manager and looking something like the organization shown in Figure 7.3.

To get a project done as quickly as possible, get a team together.

Matrix organization for a single project

A popular alternative to the project team (popular, that is, to management theorists at least) is the matrix organization. This has many forms, but the basic principle is that the project manager shares power and authority to a greater or lesser extent with some of the functional managers. We say only *some* of the functional managers because, as with team organizations, some home office administration functions, such as accounting and marketing, will lie outside the project organization. These concepts will become clearer from the illustrations, starting with Figure 7.4.

Coordination matrix

Figure 7.4 shows the principle of a coordination matrix. This kind of organization is common in manufacturing companies that are not used to dealing with projects. Their usual organization structure is simple line and function, with each manager looking after his or her own area of specialization. When a complex project hits this unsuspecting factory for the first time, the result is likely to be chaos and failure, because it has no one who can champion the project, plan it properly and see it safely through all stages from design to final test and assembly. So, when the company gets wise, it appoints a project manager for its next project and gives that person the responsibility for planning and progressing the project through all its stages to successful completion.

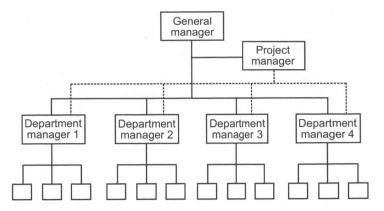

Figure 7.4 *Principle of a coordination matrix organization for one project*

In the coordination matrix, however, the project manager has absolutely no power. He or she can only coax, cajole and coordinate others to do all the project tasks. So, from the project manager's point of view at least, the matrix is weak. Unless the general manager intervenes, any department manager can use a few short well chosen words to tell the project manager exactly where to put his or her plans. So the carefully laid plans are ignored, and the project suffers.

In practice, of course, people can be tolerant and provided that everyone gets on well together the coordination matrix can see a single project through to a successful conclusion.

Matrix organizations for several simultaneous projects

Figure 7.5 takes the matrix organization a little further forward into an arrangement that can cope with more than one project at the same time. In this example the project managers each manage one of three projects, which I have called project A, project B and project C. Theoretically there is no reasonable limit to the number of projects that such a matrix could handle at the same time.

Each functional manager has groups of designers, engineers and other workers working in his or her department and must assign some of these people to work on the project managers' projects, as required. The departmental managers safeguard quality and reliability within their own specialisms and assign people to tasks. The project managers oversee planning, cost and progress control on their projects and maintain contact with the clients.

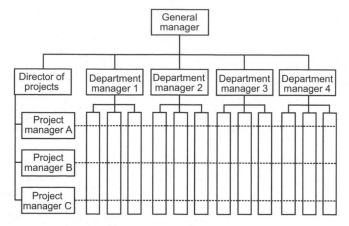

Matrix organization charts cannot show where the balance of power lies.

Figure 7.5 *Principle of a matrix organization for more than one project*

In its weakest form (not surprisingly known as the weak matrix) each project manager can only request that a departmental manager assigns people to his or her particular project. They might not get the actual people they want (by name), and it might not even be guaranteed that the same people will work on the project from one day to the next. All that depends on the discretion of the departmental managers, who are solely responsible for allocating work to people and deciding priorities between different projects.

Another form of the matrix is called the balanced matrix, in which the project managers and departmental managers have equal or balanced power. Now the project managers have a little more authority to demand what they want for their projects.

Another step up from the balanced matrix is the project matrix, in which the project manager has more power than the departmental managers and can override their decisions to some extent when there is disagreement.

The very strongest form of the matrix is the secondment matrix, in which the departmental managers must assign (or second) people to the project managers, so that those people then report directly to the project managers and only refer back to their departments if they need technical advice. The seconded people might even be asked to move to work in a project office away from their normal desks for as long as they are needed. This arrangement gets somewhere near to a team organization.

The matrix organization chart cannot show all these different strengths, so one chart does for all. It is up to senior management to decide and declare who has the greater authority. Company procedures or project procedures should make such a decision clear to everyone, so that they all know where the power and authority lie.

A matrix organization for dealing with several large projects simultaneously is shown in Figure 7.6.

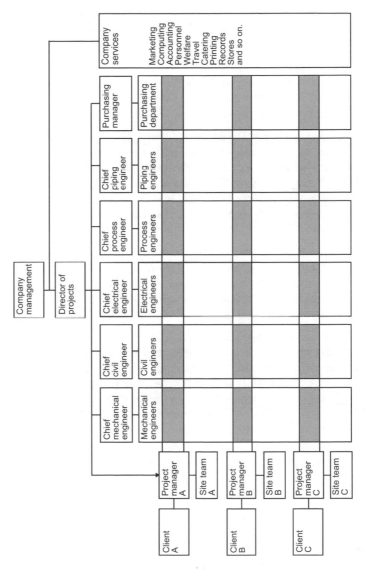

Figure 7.6 A matrix organization for a company working concurrently on three large construction projects

Advantages and disadvantages of matrix organizations

Matrix organizations have several advantages over other kinds of organization. Not the least of these is flexibility and efficiency in the deployment of home office staff. One person can flit from one project to another and back again to work on the most urgent jobs without leaving his or her desk.

Matrix organizations tend to be more stable, because they sit there permanently dealing with all the work as different projects come and go. The life of the matrix just goes on and will only end when the company decides to give up or reorganize itself.

A person working in a matrix should be able to see a career path, leading in the best case to the manager of their functional department. Stability in the organization, and working for one manager of the same specialism, means that staff appraisals and promotions are likely to be fairer. There is no air of despondency or let-down when one project comes to an end, because another project should follow in its place.

So that's all lovely – let's all go for the matrix! But hold on, wait a minute, there are some snags. With project staff dispersed over a matrix and mixed with people working on other projects, it is more difficult to establish a motivational team spirit than it is when a team actually exists.

A more serious drawback with the matrix organization is that a person working within one of the departments has two bosses, the project manager and the departmental manager. If these two managers agree, then all is well. If they don't, all is hell. It's no fun working for two managers at the same time if those managers have different ideas on the job that should be done. The matrix organization *violates the rule of unity of command*, which declares that each worker should have only one boss. (I once worked in a matrix organization where my project manager was messily divorced from my department manager's sister. It was not a pretty place to be.)

> 'No man can serve two masters: for either he will hate the one, and love the other; or else he will hold to the one and despise the other' (Matthew 6, 24).

Nevertheless, a matrix organization, with all its faults, is a very good choice for a home office organization that is handling several projects at the same time, especially when those projects are of relatively short duration.

A contract matrix for a single project

The contract matrix shown in Figure 7.7 takes a wider view of the project organization and brings in other key players besides the contractor and the client. This kind of organization is best explained by looking at what each person or company shown on the chart actually wants or does. One characteristic of the contract matrix is that many of the companies taking part in the project have enough complex work to justify employing their own project managers. So we can have a project with many project managers, but with all the subsidiary project managers having to plan and work with the main project manager to ensure that the overall project targets are achieved.

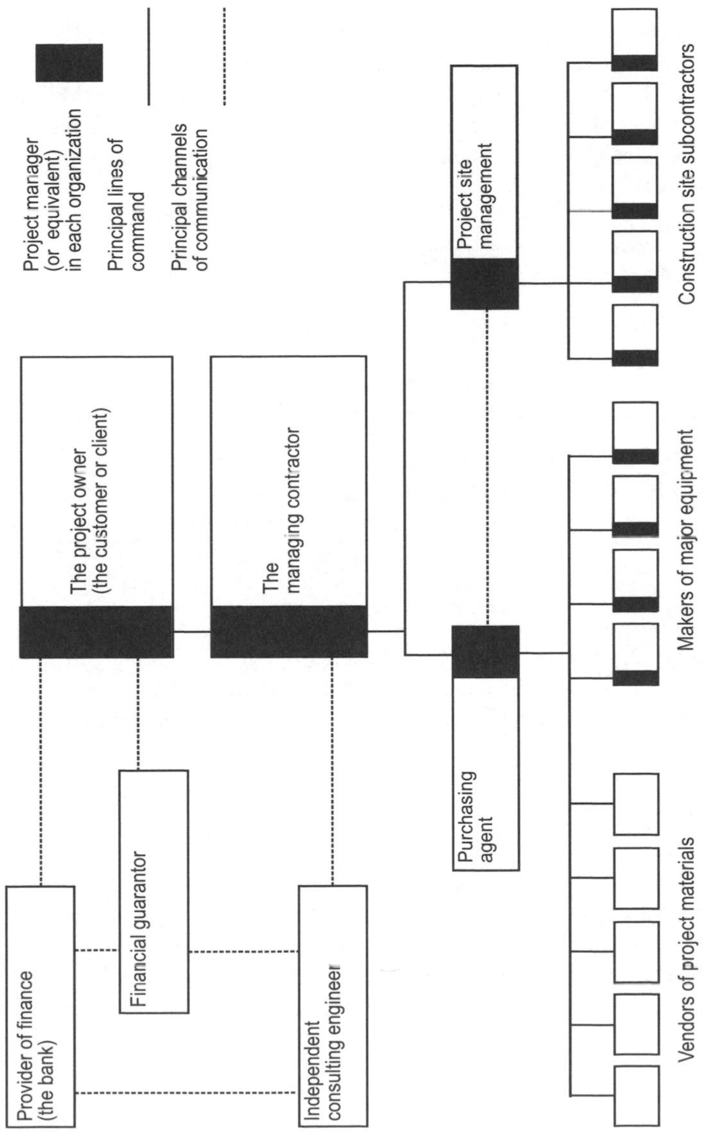

Figure 7.7 *The key players in a contract matrix*

The client

The client, or the project owner, is the company or person who wants to invest in the project. In the organization shown in Figure 7.7 it is assumed that the client has conducted a feasibility study and made a business plan that is good enough to impress the bank into lending some money to tide the owner over until the project starts to earn money and pay for itself. Perhaps it is an office building that is going to bring in rent, or a tollbridge that will eventually pay for itself from tolls charged to traffic using the bridge.

Although the client has good business sense, construction management and project management do not figure very highly in his list of skills. In fact, they probably do not figure there at all. So the owner of this project must look for professional help in getting the project planned, designed and built. That's where the managing contractor comes in.

The managing contractor

The managing contractor is a large construction company or consulting organization that has the competency to plan, design, organize and manage the project as agent for the client. It will probably have architects and design staff on its home office payroll.

The managing contractor might also have tradesmen on its payroll as direct employees, but is more likely to use subcontractors to carry out the site works, under the supervision of its site manager.

The bank

During the life of the project the client will be expected to make stage payments to the managing contractor, and, if necessary, a bank might be persuaded to provide the cash needed during the early days before the project starts to earn revenue for the client.

Stage payments are a feature in contracts of all sizes and play a large part in keeping the contractor's cash position healthy – provided that the client pays on time.

The financial guarantor

The bank will probably want some kind of guarantor to stand surety for a substantial part of the loan. The client will have to find and engage a suitable company to stand as that guarantor. For some export projects from the United Kingdom the Government's Export Credits Guarantee Department (ECGD) can sometimes fulfil this role.

The independent consulting engineer

Neither the bank nor the guarantor is likely to be technically competent to judge progress or quality as design and building take place. Almost all contracts make provision for progress or stage payments, which eventually land at the client's door for settlement. So an independent engineer is appointed who can certify at least the early claims for payment to show that the design and preparation work being claimed for has in fact been done. Later in the project, quantity surveyors will be able to measure and certify the amount of work done at the site and they will issue certificates to support claims for payment.

This engineer is not to be confused with the project engineer, who typically works under the project manager as part of the project design team, but is likely to be a separate company with the appropriate construction skills. The engineer must be seen to be independent, with no bias towards any of the parties.

The purchasing agent

The project buyer or purchasing agent will be responsible for obtaining and assessing bids for major plant and equipment purchases, might help in the negotiation of subcontracts, and will generally work with freight-forwarding companies and the suppliers to ensure that goods and materials of the right quality are delivered to site in the right quantities, at the right time and at the right price. The purchasing agent might be an independent organization but is more likely to be a department of the main contractor.

Good cooperation between the design engineers and the purchasing agent is essential if goods are to be obtained that are fit for use and at an economical price. Sometimes there is conflict between the design departments and purchasing agents, especially in the choice of vendors. Such conflict is unproductive and should be discouraged. Usually both the designers and the purchasing agent have valuable experience, and that should be combined for each purchase order to arrive at the best decisions for the project.

The purchasing agent might also be asked to assist in inspection and expediting visits to suppliers, possibly accompanied by design engineers or inspectors from the main contractor. For some international projects the managing contractor might appoint more than one purchasing agent, based strategically around the world, ready to carry out local inspection and expediting duties.

Vendors of project materials

Not much need be said here about the vendors of construction materials, since every construction manager should be familiar with their ordering and supply. Some rare materials or bulk purchases, such as structural steel, might need special attention from the purchasing agent, but this should be a fairly routine procedure.

Makers of major equipment

Some large projects, such as the petrochemical and mining industries or projects for the construction of power-generating plant, might include the design and manufacture of items such as cranes, locomotives, heavy machinery, huge turbines and electrical generators and so on. As the design and manufacture of any such item is a project in its own right, each manufacturer will be expected to have a project manager working with a suitable set of planning and progressing procedures. The purchasing agent (and possibly also the managing contractor) might want to make sure that such procedures exist before placing each order.

Construction site manager

The site manager will usually be an employee of the managing contractor who reports back to the project manager or, in some cases, to a home office-based construction director. The site manager of a very large project has a very senior role to play and, at the peak of activity, might be compared with the chief executive of a small town. Certainly, in some very large projects on virgin territory, the site manager might have to build an airstrip, construct major access roads, supply housing for all grades of staff and visitors, set up a hospital, and so on, all over and above building the actual project.

Coming back down to earth, to more medium-sized projects, the site manager might preside over an organization with the functions shown in Figure 7.8.

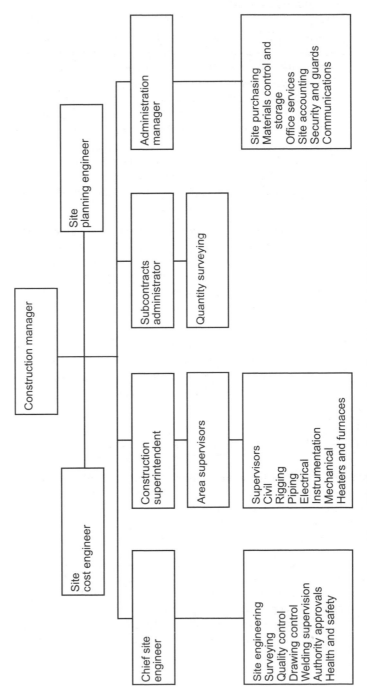

Figure 7.8 *Elements of a construction site organization for a large project*

Hybrid organizations

The organizations described so far are basic forms, and there are usually wide variations seen in practice. Most companies have organizations that are, at first sight, so complex that they are difficult to analyse and put into a category. However, we can describe one common variant here, which is when a company operates a matrix organization for most of its projects but sets up project teams for special cases. This arrangement is best explained by two real-life cases, both of which concerned a mining engineering company in London that was generally organized like the matrix shown in Figure 7.6. This company had two fairly large projects that each fell into the specialism of a single department, as follows:

1 A reclamation programme was needed to recover some flooded underground workings, where a tragic accident had happened some years previously. This project consisted almost entirely of providing batteries of slurry pumps and pipes. So a project team was set up to design and manage the project from the London office, with the chief piping engineer acting as project manager.

2 The second special team project was for the supply and installation of a very big electrical transformer. As practically all the design work was electrical, all the work was assigned to a small team within the electrical department, with the chief electrical engineer acting as project manager.

Joint venture organizations

There are occasions when the amount of project investment needed is too high for one company to risk or provide, or where a project needs multiple skills that no single company possesses. In such cases two or more companies, who might in other circumstances be competitors, get together to bid for the project as a joint venture.

If the bid is successful, a joint venture project company is set up specially to design and build the project. The joint venture company's board and management will probably contain representatives seconded from each of the constituent companies. The project manager will most likely report to the joint venture company's board and will preside over a dedicated project team.

Organizing project procedures: the project manual or handbook

Companies embarking on large projects usually have a range of procedures available to them for project management. Not every project needs all the procedures, so a decision must be made at or very near the project start to decide which of the many possible procedures will apply to the new project.

When deciding on the project organization and on who will do what in the project, it is useful to set out the decisions in a responsibility matrix chart, such as that shown in Figure 7.9. This lists the kinds of task or decision to be made during the project and, against that list, shows who will be primarily responsible for carrying out the task, those who must assist with secondary responsibility and those who must be consulted before the task can be signed off. The responsibility chart can be included in the project manual.

Some companies prepare a similar chart, called a document distribution matrix, to show the primary distribution requirements for important hard-copy documents.

Task type:	The client	Project manager	Project engineer	Purchasing manager	Drawing office	Construction manager	Planning engineer	Cost engineer	Project accountant	and so on.
Make designs			+	●						
Approve designs	●	■	+							
Purchase enquiries		■	+	●						
Purchase orders	■	■	+	●						
Planning	■	■	+	+	+	+	●	+		
Cost control		●		+		+		+		
Progress reports		●	+	+	+	+	+			
Cost reports		●		+		+		+	+	
and so on.										

● Principal responsibility (only one per task)
+ Secondary responsibility
■ Must be consulted

Figure 7.9 *A responsibility matrix chart*

Other contents of a typical project manual include contact details for all managers in the organization, including subcontractors, so that people working on the project, the client and secretaries know where and how to contact all the key people and companies. Summary and detailed organization charts, showing how all the key people and companies relate to each other, are usually included too.

Chapter 8

Risk Management

Do you remember the UFO shopping mall project from Chapter 5? That was to be built over a plague pit and a gasworks, so we have some idea of the nasties that awaited the earthmovers. But suppose that, when the existing buildings have been demolished and the excavators really get going, we uncover a Roman temple. Once the local archaeological society, university and a few history preservation bodies get to hear about this wonderful find the main contractor can expect much of the project to come to a dead stop. The big diggers will fall silent, and little diggers on hands and knees with trowels in their fists will take their place for a month or two. So here's a pretty kettle of fish: a completely unforeseen and (some would say) unforeseeable project delay of perhaps several months. Unexpected delays are always possible in projects, and learning to anticipate and deal with them is all part of risk management, which in turn is a part of project strategy.

A kettle of fish can never be pretty.

Know your enemy: what are the risks?

The first stage in risk management is to think about the risks that your project might suffer. Bad weather is an obvious choice. Materials shortages, labour disputes, design errors are others. Less likely, at least on mainland Britain, are earthquakes, hurricanes and similar natural disasters, but flooding might be a possibility in some places. So, how do we go about listing all the risks, including the likely risks, the less likely risks and the bizarre outsiders?

There are at least two ways of approaching this problem. The first is to refer to checklists. These can grow in size and value as companies gain more project experience, and are usually a good starting point for listing the foreseeable risks. Checklists can play an important part in many aspects of project management, such as feasibility studies, preparing business plans, project definition, cost estimating, buying software, start-up activities and many more.

The second method that can be tried is brainstorming. This has nothing to do with mental illness. It simply means getting a group of people together to milk their collective minds for ideas and imagination. A very comprehensive risk list can be made this way. For a brainstorming meeting, several people, chosen for their knowledge and experience, are asked to meet for an hour or two in the presence of a trained person (let's call that person the 'leader'). People at the meeting are encouraged to suggest any possible risks that they can imagine for the particular project. No suggestion should be rejected at this stage as being too outrageous. If someone suggests an attack by aliens, take it on board for the moment. The leader should encourage an atmosphere of 'anything goes', so that participants feel free to propose even the most bizarre risks without fear of ridicule. Every suggestion is written down on flipchart sheets. You might need several flipchart sheets before the meeting is finished.

Two minds are better than one, but three are better still.

This chapter assumes that brainstorming will be used to make the initial risk list. It's probably the best way.

Classifying risks

Once all the possible risks have been listed, the project manager or risk expert then goes through the list and strikes out any suggestions that really are beyond the bounds of possibility. We are then left with a list of possible events, either likely or improbable, that could damage the project. If the brainstorming people have done their job well, this will be a very long list.

No project manager could cope with every possible threat, so we need to classify each risk according to how seriously it might affect the project. We also need to know how likely the risk is to happen. The risk of the project manager being struck by lightning might be one in a million, but would be a serious risk setback to the project. An earthquake in Surbiton is not likely, but if one did happen and it left the project home office as a heap of rubble, it would be somewhat inconvenient to say the least. Heavy rain might stop construction work only for a short time and cause no lasting damage but is far more probable than the extremely unlikely earthquake. (If, as you read this, you feel the earth move, ornaments fall off the mantelpiece and cracks appear in the ceiling, I'm sorry but that's just Sod's Law.)

The odds are much shorter if the project manager is a keen golfer.

Figure 8.1 shows a chart that categorizes risks in this fairly simple way. The results indicate how we might regard each risk and, where necessary, plan to minimize any possible effects. Risks with very low potential and a low chance of happening might be ignored completely. High-impact, high-probability risks must be given serious consideration, and we shall need to have action plans in place to deal with them in case the worst happens. So we could compile a list classified under the headings suggested by Figure 8.1.

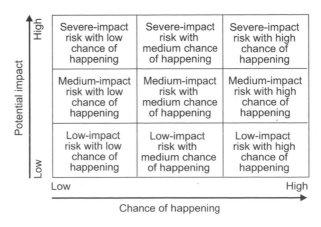

Figure 8.1 *One kind of risk classification matrix*

A simpler version containing only the following headings, can be used:

- high chance – high impact
- high chance – low impact
- low chance – high impact
- low chance – low impact

Now we are beginning to develop a risk management strategy. One important aspect of this strategy must be to recognize that the bad effects of risks tend to get worse towards the middle and end of the project. This is because as the project progresses, more and more time and money has been put into it (the so-called sunk costs) and there will be more investment at stake if risk events cause scrap and rework, or even project abandonment. Putting it another way, a risk happening in the first few weeks of a project might mean scrapping a few drawings or other papers, but a disaster near the end of the project could involve tearing the building down and starting all over again. We have all seen examples of mistakes made during construction and initial design errors that were not discovered until the building was nearly finished.

Make sure that all designs have been checked. Architects are not perfect. When it's time to do the work, measure twice – cut once.

All this suggests another way of classifying risks, perhaps within each of the categories already seen in Figure 8.1:

1 Risks most likely to occur at the start of the project.
2 Risks most likely to occur during the execution of the project.
3 Risks that can affect the final stages of a project, particularly during commissioning.
4 Risks occurring during the initial period of project operation, after handover to the customer.
5 Risks that can occur at any time in the project.

Putting priorities on different kinds of risk

A practical way of classifying risks is to rank them according to the probability of their occurrence and the severity of the impact if they should occur. For this, it is necessary to start by considering the possible causes and effects of every risk.

There are methods, borrowed from quality assurance practitioners, that can help in ranking the risks. Chief among these methods are failure mode and effect analysis (FMEA) and failure mode, effect and criticality analysis (FMECA).

Failure mode and effect analysis (FMEA)

FMEA analysis is a method for writing down anticipated risk events, then considering the severity of the risk occurrence, and looking at possible measures that might be taken.

Item		Failure mode	Cause of failure	Effect	Recommended action
Main building floors	1.1	Building collapses during installation of heavy machinery.	Errors in floor loading calculations.	Personal injuries. Project delays. Damaged machines.	Arrange for calculations to be checked in future.
	1.2	Building collapses during installation of heavy machinery.	Floor concrete incorrectly poured.	Personal injuries. Project delays. Damaged machines.	Employ competent site engineering manager.
Security lighting	2.1	Some lights not operating.	Lamps burned out after only 100 hours.	Reduced site security. Risk of personal accident.	Choose best quality lamps. Ensure correct voltage rating. Consider sodium lamps for longer life.
	2.2	All lights fail to come on at correct times.	Faulty timeswitches.	Reduced site security. Risk of personal accident. Risk of fire in switchroom.	Use reliable brand of timer. Ensure contacts correctly rated. Ensure correct circuit protection.
Roof	3.1	Roof sheets flap in high wind.	Fixings wrongly installed.	Risk of injury. Ingress of rain.	Check all fixings and replace if necessary.
	3.2	Roof sheets flap in high wind.	Fixing intervals too great.	Risk of injury. Ingress of rain.	Install more fixings.

Table 8.1 *Failure mode and effect analysis (FMEA)*

Table 8.1 shows part of a simple FMEA chart. Item 1 in this example considers structural failure risks in the floors of a new building for a manufacturing plant or other processing facility. The scope of this project includes designing and constructing the building, and then installing and commissioning all the plant and machinery. The point about the FMEA analysis is that it must be done before building starts, so that the risk events predicted don't actually happen.

During the initial brainstorming meeting, one person has asked what would happen if a floor structure were to collapse during or after the installation of some of the very heavy machinery required for this project. The chart analyses possible causes of the risk event and then looks at the consequences. The right-hand column of the chart records actions that can be taken to prevent the failure or to mitigate the effects if it should happen.

Other entries in Table 8.1 are self-explanatory and need no further comment. On a project of significant size the FMEA chart might have a large number of entries.

This is a *qualitative* process, which means that risks are considered only in descriptive terms with no attempt to put numbers on anything. The characteristics of each risk are examined, but the risks are not ranked according to their possible degree of severity. This means that a first glance at the chart might indicate that the failure of an electric lamp on a perimeter road would be just as significant as the collapse of a floor in the building.

Thus we need to carry risk analysis forward to take account of the possible severity. This can concentrate the minds of managers on the risks that pose the greatest threat. We could do this by *quantitative* analysis, of which failure mode, effect and criticality analysis is a common method.

Failure mode, effect and criticality analysis (FMECA)

Quantitative analysis methods attempt to assign numerical values to risks and their possible effects. They often examine the probable impact on project time and costs. Alternatively, the evaluation process can produce a ranking number for every identified risk. Risks with a high-ranking number should have first claim for management attention and expenditure on preventive measures.

FMECA is one step further on from the FMEA method just described and illustrated in Table 8.1. The main difference is that we now try to put some numbers on each risk that will help indicate its possible severity and ranking. An example is shown in Table 8.2. Note that this FMECA chart has three columns in which the assessor can award a mark of seriousness (in this case on a scale of 1 to 10). The higher numbers indicate the greatest risk.

Item		Failure mode	Cause of failure	Effect	Chance	Severity	Detection difficulty	Rank
Main building floors	1.1	Building collapses during installation of heavy machinery.	Errors in floor loading calculations.	Personal injuries Project delays Damaged machines	2	10	9	180
	1.2	Building collapses during installation of heavy machinery.	Floor concrete incorrectly poured.	Personal injuries Project delays Damaged machines	3	10	10	300
Security lighting	2.1	Some lights not operating.	Lamps burned out after only 100 hours.	Reduced site security Risk of personal accident	1	4	1	4
	2.2	All lights fail to come on at correct times.	Faulty timeswitches.	Reduced site security Risk of personal accident Risk of fire in switchroom	2	5	1	10
Roof	3.1	Roof sheets flap in high wind.	Fixings wrongly installed.	Risk of injury Ingress of rain	2	5	4	40
	3.2	Roof sheets flap in high wind.	Fixing intervals too great.	Risk of injury Ingress of rain	1	5	3	15

Table 8.2 Failure mode, effect and criticality analysis (FMECA)

The risk events shown in Table 8.2 are the same as those included in the FMEA example of Table 8.1. Looking at item 1.1, the assessor clearly thinks that this event is unlikely to happen because she has ranked chance as 2, at the lower end of the 1 to 10 scale. There is no doubt, however, that if this event did occur it would be extremely serious, so the degree of severity has been marked as 10.

Detection difficulty means the difficulty of noticing the cause of this risk in time to take preventive action. In this case it refers specifically to the difficulty in spotting a design error before the concrete floors are poured.

Each risk event is given a ranking number by multiplying the scores in the chance, severity and detection difficulty columns. The problem with any such method is that all the results are based on guesswork or best judgements, and the final ranking factors can be misleading.

Common sense

When ranking risks in order of priority, although FMEA and FMECA methods can help, they are not essential. Plain common sense must be the real guide.

So, to sum up what we have done so far towards developing our risk strategy, we have:

- used brainstorming to list all possible and impossible risks
- edited the list obtained from brainstorming to remove the most bizarre ideas
- sorted the remaining risk possibilities so that those needing most attention are moved to the top of the list.

Risk countermeasures

When all the known risks have been listed, assessed and ranked, it is time to consider what might be done about them. The project manager has a range of options, including the following six:

1 avoid the risk
2 take precautions to prevent the risk or reduce its impact
3 accept the risk
4 share the risk with others in a joint venture
5 limit the contractor's liability
6 transfer the risk by taking out insurance.

Risk avoidance

The only way to avoid a risk altogether is to abandon the work associated with the possible cause or find a different way of doing the work. In extreme cases this might mean deciding not to undertake the project at all.

Taking precautions

Taking precautions to prevent a risk or reduce its effects is a most important part of risk management. It needs high-level risk prevention strategy and management determination to ensure that all preventive measures are always followed throughout all parts of the organization. Here are a just a few examples of many possible practical measures, listed in no particular sequence, some applying to small projects and others to larger projects:

A final artificial task (perhaps with a duration of four weeks) can be put in the network diagram as a safety buffer to take up bad weather delays.

- erect site security fencing to reduce the chance of equipment and materials thefts and vandalism
- provide one or more secure, lockable site huts
- get the roof on as quickly as possible, so that dry trades can work when it rains
- calculate the statistical chance of bad weather, and then allow extra time in the plan
- regularly inspect and test electrical equipment and other tools to ensure safe operation
- double-check for errors in design calculations for vital project components or structures
- provide back-up electrical power supplies for vital operations
- give on-the-job training so that back-up staff can understudy key roles in the organization
- regularly inspect and maintain lifts and hoists
- provide safety clothing and equipment and enforce their use
- restrict access to hazardous areas
- choose the time of year most likely to provide fair weather for outdoor projects
- give adequate training to all who operate potentially hazardous tools and machinery
- arrange regular financial audits and the installation of procedures to identify or deter fraud.

Risk acceptance

There are many small things than can go wrong during the course of any project, and most of these risks can be accepted in the knowledge that their effect is not likely to be serious and that they can be dealt with by on-the-spot corrections or some slight replanning. Good attention to design detail, followed by efficient purchasing and site supervision, can eliminate many of these small inconveniences.

There will be other risks that, though potentially severe, are not very likely to happen and will have to be accepted because no effective countermeasures can be taken.

Risk sharing

If a project, or a big part of it, appears to carry a very high risk, the contractor might look for one or more external partners to undertake the work as a joint venture. These external companies might even be competitors for other project work. Sharing reduces the impact of any failure on the individual companies in the partnership. Sharing a risk big enough to ruin one company might reduce its impact to little more than a temporary inconvenience when two or three are sharing the work and the obligations.

Risk limitation

There are times when project risks should only be accepted if safeguards can be put in place to limit their potential effect. This might mean having some sort of escape clause in the contract that gives the contractor an opportunity to pull out of the contract or levy extra charges on the client if some unplanned event happens that is not the contractor's fault. Provisional sums in cost estimates are an example of risk limitation.

Risk transference through insurance

Some risks, or substantial parts of them, can be transferred to another party on payment of a fee or premium. This leads to the important subject of insurance, which is discussed in the section below.

Insurance

The financial impact of many risks can be offset by insuring against them. The client pays the insurance company a premium for this service. The insurer might choose to spread the risk further by sharing it with one or more other insurance companies. Figure 8.2 shows that managers do not have complete freedom of choice when deciding which risks should be insured.

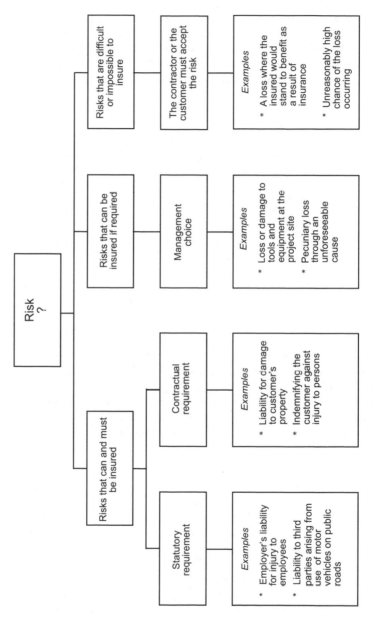

Figure 8.2 *Risk and insurance in project management*

Categories of insurance

There are four main classes of insurance:

1 legal liabilities (payments to others as a result of statutory, contractual or professional commitments, compensation awarded by the courts, legal expenses (but not fines imposed by the courts)
2 protection against loss or damage to property, including work in progress
3 cover relating to personnel
4 pecuniary loss.

An insurance policy may combine cover for two or more of the above classes of risk.

Legally required insurances

At the top of the insurance shopping list are those items which must be insured in order to comply with laws and regulations. Third-party insurance for motor vehicles used on public roads is a familiar example. Employers are obliged to insure their employees against injury or illness arising from their employment (employers' liability insurance), and every employer has to display a valid certificate on noticeboards to show that such insurance exists.

Statutory regulations of particular interest to the managers of construction and engineering projects cover the periodic inspection and certification of lifting equipment, pressure systems and local-exhaust ventilation plant. No project which includes the installation of such equipment should be handed over to a client without the relevant written (or other) scheme of examination and inspection certificates. If the correct documents are not supplied, the client will not legally be able to operate the equipment.

In the UK these regulations form part of the Health and Safety at Work Act 1974. Much of this legislation resulted from European directives, and similar legislation has been enacted in other EU member countries. The inspection work is usually done by engineer-surveyors employed by an engineering insurance company that will probably be engaged by the main contractor. The larger of these insurance companies, with many years' experience of such work, arc ablc to advisc on compliance with national and local legislation covering equipment and construction materials.

The project or site manager must check that inspection certificates required by the regulations are current and valid for plant hired for use on a construction site. This will help protect the project manager's organization from any liability that might arise from the use of a plant hire fleet that has been poorly managed by the plant hire company.

In construction projects the contractor will almost certainly be asked to insure against several risks. All the model terms of contract from the electrical, chemical, civil and professional institutions embody such requirements. The main contractor will also wish to make certain that subcontractors are bound, in turn, by similar conditions.

Liability insurances are most likely to feature prominently in project contracts. The project purchaser will want to know, for example, that the contractor has adequate cover for legal liability in the event of personal injury, illness or death caused to anyone as a result of the project.

In summary, liability insurances may be required for:

- compensation to persons for bodily harm (employees of either party, others working on site, visitors and members of the public)
- property loss or damage, including work in progress
- financial loss
- infringement of property rights
- accidents
- product liability (arising from the use of a product)
- professional negligence
- nuisance caused by the works
- environmental damage.

Every organization or professional person with project responsibility (including architects, consultants, surveyors, designers and project management organizations) must make certain that they have adequate professional liability insurance to cover any liability that they might incur in the course of their work.

Other risks that can be covered by insurance

In addition to the statutory and contractual requirements, there is a range of other risks against which a contractor might be required to insure, or for which a contractor might decide that insurance is prudent. Some of these are listed below.

Contractors' all risks insurance for construction and engineering projects

All risks insurance cover provides protection during the works, until the project is complete and handed over to the customer. Thereafter, insurance becomes the customer's responsibility.

All risks policies typically protect work in progress against fire, storm damage, theft and malicious damage, but any new policy proposal should be studied with care as it is likely to list exceptions. In addition to work in progress, the cover should include loss or damage to:

- construction plant and machinery
- hired plant
- construction materials in transit to the site
- temporary buildings and site huts
- employees' tools and effects.

Reinstatement costs after an accident will also be covered, including the costs of removing debris and the fees of architects, surveyors and consulting engineers. The insurer might also agree to pay additional expenses (such as overtime costs and express carriage rates) incurred as a result of expediting reinstatement work.

Contract all risks (CAR) policies usually apply to civil engineering and construction projects, while the less common engineering all risks (EAR) policies are for contracts that relate specifically to the construction and installation of machinery.

Decennial (latent defects) insurance

Decennial insurance, which can cover a period of up to ten years, is designed to insure against damage to premises caused specifically by an inherent defect in the design, materials or construction of a project. In the event of a successful claim, decennial insurance removes the need for the project owner to suffer the expense of taking legal action for recompense against the contractor.

Accident and sickness insurance

Provisions for personal accident, sickness and medical expenses insurance will need particular consideration when employees are required to travel, whether at home or abroad. Those working on projects in foreign countries will expect to be adequately covered for the higher risks involved, and such cover will have to be extended to spouses and children if they are also allowed to travel.

Key person insurance

Key person insurance (which, until the aficionados of political correctness had their way, used to be called key man insurance) offers various kinds of protection to an employer against expenses or loss of profits which result when illness, injury or death prevents one or more named key people from performing the duties expected of them. Arrangements are flexible, and policies can be tailored to suit particular circumstances.

Pecuniary insurance

Pecuniary insurances are designed to protect a company against financial losses from a variety of causes. Risks that can be covered include embezzlement, loss through interruption of business and legal expenses. In some limited circumstances, advance profits insurance may be possible to provide cover for delay in receiving planned return on project investment caused by the late completion of the project.

Of particular interest to contractors where business with foreign clients is involved is export credit insurance. In the UK, the government's Export Credits Guarantee Department (ECGD) provides guarantees that can provide security against bank loans for large capital goods and long-term projects. Most industrialized companies have similar schemes. The contractor will be expected to bear some of the risk, although his proportion will usually be small. The security offered by credit insurance can be an important factor in obtaining finance for a project.

Risks which cannot be covered by insurance

There are risks which an underwriter will either refuse to insure, or for which the premium demanded would be prohibitive. Such cases arise in the following circumstances:

- Where the chances against a loss occurring are too high or, in other words, where the risk is seen as more of a certainty than reasonable chance. Examples are losses made through speculative trading or because of disadvantageous changes in foreign exchange rates.
- Where the insurer is not able to spread its risk over a sufficient number of similar risks.
- Where the insurer does not have access to sufficient data from the past to be able to quantify the future risk.
- Where the insured would stand to gain as a result of a claim. Except in some forms of personal insurance, the principle of insurance is to attempt to reinstate the insured's position to that which existed before the loss event. A person cannot, for example, expect to benefit personally from a claim for loss or damage to property not belonging to him or her (property in which he or she has no *insurable interest*).

These items must, therefore, be excluded from the insurance portfolio. In some cases, other commercial remedies might exist for offsetting the risks.

Obtaining insurance

Insurance can be sought directly from an underwriter or through a broker – preferably one with a good reputation and experience in the insured's type of project activity. The insurer will need to be supplied with sufficient information for the risk to be adequately defined, and the contractor will be expected to inform the insurer of any change of circumstances likely to affect the risks insured. The insurer may wish to make investigations or even follow up the project work using its own experts.

Professional advice from insurers can often be of great benefit in reducing risks, especially in the areas of health and safety and crime prevention.

Following fairly recent political and commercial disasters, some insurers have had their fingers badly burned or have even been forced out of business. So it is not surprising that insurers in general have become more particular about issuing policies, assessing the risks and the premiums charged. Liability insurance, for example, has become expensive. Employer's liability cover, even though it is a legal requirement in the UK, is becoming difficult to obtain. Some insurance companies have had to close because they are unable to effect such insurance. Therefore, it is now more important than ever for a project manager to involve an insurance specialist at a very early planning stage, in case he or she should find out, at a later stage, that insurance cover is not available at short notice.

Statistical methods for dealing with uncertainty in plans and cost budgets

All plans and budgets are based on estimates, and those estimates are our best judgements on what should happen if everything goes to plan. But, of course, things do not always go exactly to plan. So, for many reasons, the final times and costs might turn out to be somewhat different from those that we predicted at the start of the project. Some people like to make statistical predictions of the probable outcome of their projects, starting from the fact that they are not confident about their time and cost estimates.

We shall deal mainly with time estimates here, but the same methods can be applied to cost estimate uncertainties.

Program evaluation and review technique (PERT)

Ever since the early days of critical path network analysis some people have regarded uncertainty or inaccuracy in estimating task durations as a problem. Consequently, one of the most common early methods of network analysis tried to overcome this difficulty by allowing the estimator some latitude. This method was called program evaluation and review technique, and its acronym, PERT, has often been wrongly applied to critical path analysis in general ever since those early days. No one really cares about that, but the following gives the true story of PERT.

PERT is a critical path network planning method in which it is recognized that all task duration estimates are at risk and might, in practice, take a shorter or longer time than the planner intended. With PERT, therefore, the planner is given the luxury of being able to make three duration estimates for every task:

t_o = the most *optimistic* duration that could be foreseen

t_m = the most *likely* duration (which is the estimate that normally would be made)

t_p = the most *pessimistic* duration

These three estimates are used to produce a probable duration (the expected *time) for each task, using the following simple formula:*

$$t_e = \frac{t_o + 4t_m + t_p}{6}$$

(where t_e is the expected time)

This calculation is repeated for every task in the network. Then time analysis is carried out, using only the *expected* times.

Using a computer for PERT

The speed and power of modern computers allows us to take a more sophisticated approach to PERT. This is sometimes called the Monte Carlo method, and it works like this. The input data to the project management software, as in PERT, comes from a network diagram in which estimates for the most likely durations of tasks are supplemented by estimates for the most optimistic and most pessimistic times. The computer is then asked to perform time analysis repeatedly for, perhaps 200, 500 or even 1000 times. For each time analysis calculation the computer selects, at random, a different combination of the optimistic, pessimistic and most likely duration estimates for all the tasks.

At one extreme, therefore, the computer is likely to carry out a calculation in which all the optimistic task durations have been selected, and this will give the earliest possible completion time for the project. At the other extreme, one or more calculations will occur in which the computer has used all the most pessimistic times, so that the result is the most pessimistic forecast for the project completion date.

In between these two extremes, depending on the number of time analysis calculations performed, there will be a range of forecasts for project completion with a large number of combinations of optimistic, pessimistic and most likely duration estimates. The computer will usually make the calculation in the twinkling of an eye, but very large networks might take a second or two.

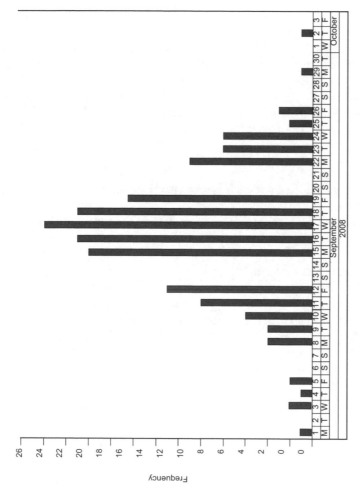

Figure 8.3 Predictions for a project finish date using Monte Carlo analysis

The result of Monte Carlo analysis is usually printed out by the computer as a graph similar to that shown in Figure 8.3 although I have redrawn and edited this heavily for clarity. The project used for this example had about 25 tasks and was very similar to the workshop project first described in Chapter 2. The computer made about 175 repeat time analysis calculations to arrive at this result. The left-hand scale gives the number of results falling on each particular date. We see that there is a slight possibility of the project being finished by 1 September 2008 and also a very slight possibility that the project will not be finished before 2 October 2008. The peak of the graph shows that the expected time for finishing this project is 17 September 2008.

Notice that no results are scheduled on weekend dates, because this project was planned using a five-day week calendar.

This example was calculated using a program called OPERA, which is part of the OPEN PLAN suite of project management programs. Many other modern programs can do the same job. There is no reason why the same method, using the same kind of software, should not be used to predict project costs. All that is needed is to supply three cost estimates for some or all of the activities in the project and then select those data for the analysis.

Tailpiece

Many successful project managers will go through their entire working lives without using PERT, FMEA or FMECA methods. These techniques have been described in this chapter more because they exist than because they are vital tools. So, if all this seems a bit strange and beyond what you had been led to expect, don't despair. Remember that risk management, along with most other project management topics, is all about common sense. So, to sum up, if you are to deal with risks effectively, you must:

1 list all the possible risks you can think of
2 decide which risks are the most likely and the most important
3 take advice and decide what insurance policies you must have
4 decide what you can do to minimize risk damage to your project.

Chapter 9

Controlling Project Costs

126

Much that is written about project cost control is really about project cost collection and reporting. Although cost accounting and reporting are essential for several operational and legal reasons, these procedures can only report costs that have already been incurred. None of this is called *historical costing* for nothing. Once too much has been spent, it's probably too late to do much about it. The time for cost control action is *before* the money is spent, not afterwards. This chapter needs to be read with that principle in mind, but all project managers must nevertheless work closely with their project or company accountants. Project managers have to appreciate the nature of project costs, and know how those costs are estimated, recorded and reported. Then we can start to think about how to control them.

Important project health warning! Cost reporting is fine for history students, but it is not cost control.

A brief introduction to project accounting

If you are a self-employed builder, working with one or two family members and doing all the management yourself, you will probably be working on just one or two projects, with perhaps more work waiting in the pipeline. Project accounting, although it might be a terrible time-wasting nuisance, is fairly straightforward. As a good honest citizen you simply record all your allowable expenses in one ledger and all your income in another. When self-assessment time comes you make up and file your tax return, and that's it for another year.

If your business expands and you find yourself running a head office and several construction jobs on a number of diverse sites, you will need to take cost and management accounting far more seriously. So this chapter begins with a short explanation of project cost accounting. Details vary from one company to another, but there are a few fundamentals that should apply to every organization.

Direct and indirect costs

In the case of the tiny firm with just one job going at a time, all costs incurred can be charged to that job. No problem. We call those costs *direct costs* because they can be associated directly with the project. They are also called *variable costs*, because their amount varies with the amount of work done.

With a larger company, the costs at each project site can still be charged direct to the relevant project. But home office costs are not quite so easy to deal with. Figure 9.1 sets out the way in which costs can be classified in the larger company.

Some home office costs are concerned with administration, keeping the building and its services running and so on. Those costs cannot easily be charged to individual projects and are sometimes called *indirect* costs or *overheads*. They also tend to be *fixed* costs,

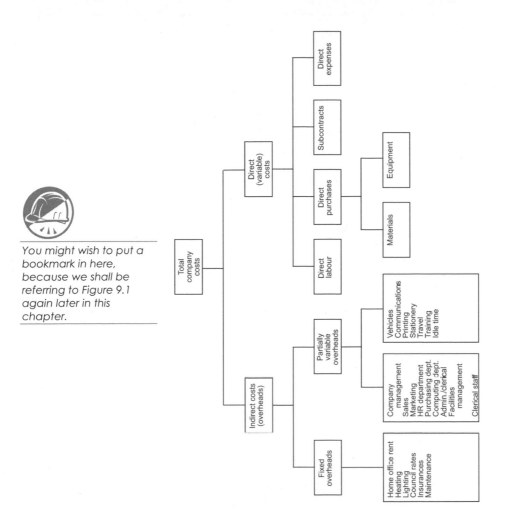

You might wish to put a bookmark in here, because we shall be referring to Figure 9.1 again later in this chapter.

Figure 9.1 *A simplified comparison of indirect and direct company costs*

because the company's headquarters and administrative staff have to be kept going whatever the level of work in hand. So the costs don't vary much with the construction workload.

Indirect costs usually include sales and marketing, the costs of submitting proposals to prospective clients for new work, accommodation costs, salaries of directors and some senior managers, clerical workers, communications and so on. Companies typically recover these indirect costs (overheads) by adding a percentage to their direct costs, so that when they charge the client, the bill is a mix of direct costs, overhead recovery and fees or profit margin. This is called *absorption costing*. Your company will be in financial trouble if it doesn't get as much new direct work as it expects because then there will be insufficient income for recovering all the overhead costs.

Cost estimating

Initial cost estimates

All people who run small company construction businesses have to learn how to estimate project costs. That's probably one of the first things they ever have to do because, without proper cost management, they will not survive in business. So, unlike other industries, the construction industry in general has relatively good expertise in estimating direct project costs. Architects and project managers can get considerable help from published tables of typical construction project costs (notably the annually updated price books from Spon, the London publisher). Estimating is always subject to error, but it is far easier to estimate the tangible parts of a building contract than it is to estimate, say, the design of new computer software.

Now think about the basic elements of a typical cost estimate. Let's say that this is an estimate made by a contractor so that he can price a construction project proposal for a client. The estimate will break down into two main parts, which are above-the-line items and (yes, you've guessed it) below-the-line items.

Above-the-line cost items

Estimates for direct project costs can usually be summarized under the following headings:

- direct labour (which may include design costs)
- direct expenses (which include fees paid to external consultants or architects)
- purchases and subcontracts
- an allowance for overheads (the amount of which must be decided by the accountant).

A line can be ruled under these costs, which can then be added together to arrive at the total estimated cost of the project.

Below-the-line allowances

All estimators should recognize that their work is prone to errors and omissions. So we must try to make allowance for these risks by adding some extra items below the line drawn under the basic project cost estimate. The following three items commonly appear below the line in project estimates:

1 *Contingency sum.* This is a small allowance, usually calculated as a percentage of the above-the-line sum, to cover the possible errors and omissions in the estimate. The amount added in this way depends on the assessed degree of risk (a large

contingency sum is needed for high risk) and how tight price competition is for the project (you can't afford a big contingency sum if the competition is fierce). It might be five or ten per cent.

2   *Cost escalation allowance*. In times of high inflation, the contractor might attempt to add an allowance for future rises in the prices of labour and materials. This only applies for projects that are expected to last for more than a year or so.

3   *Provisional sums*. It is not always possible to define every aspect of a project before work starts. The bidding contractor might reserve the right to charge extra for prespecified items that can only be defined properly after the project has started. Suppose, for example, that the client has asked the contractor to retain all the old roof beams in a barn conversion, but some of the beams are above a plaster ceiling which potential contractors have no right to damage until they have won the contract. This means that the beams cannot be inspected for insect and rot damage before the project starts. A contractor bidding for this project might want to add a provisional sum for renewing one or more beams if these should be found structurally unsafe when they are eventually uncovered.

Pricing the project

For some small engineering projects pricing is just a question of adding up the direct costs and then adding a standard proportion as gross profit margin. Not much will be said here about pricing larger construction projects because the pricing strategy for these is complex and not easily defined. It is not simply a question of putting some straightforward level of mark-up on the cost estimates. Some projects will allow a greater gross profit margin than others. In extreme cases, projects might even have to be taken on at unprofitable prices (which means making a loss) simply to keep the permanent staff gainfully employed and together as a team until the next profitable project opportunity comes along. But that strategy can lead downhill on a steep, slippery slope to disaster if it is overdone.

What is certain, however, is that those who have to make pricing decisions will appreciate full and accurate cost estimates. The lower the degree of uncertainty in the estimates, the closer the price-setters can set their profit margins, with confidence, in the face of strong competition.

Different estimating accuracies

Project cost estimates can be made at any time during the life of a project. An estimate made near the end of a project will be more accurate than one made in the beginning, because the later estimate will contain a substantial proportion of actual recorded costs. It can be useful to classify estimates according to their expected accuracy, and here is one company's idea on this subject. The classes are listed in increasing order of accuracy.

- *Ballpark estimates*. These are early informed guesses made when virtually no drawings exist. They rely on the estimator's experience and memory of past projects of similar size. This kind of overall estimate is sometimes called top-down estimating.

- *Comparative estimates*. Comparative estimates are made by comparing costs for parts of the new project with actual recorded costs of similar project parts from the recent past. Those comparisons can give some idea of the new project's probable cost but some design work will have to have been done before the estimates can be finished. The best comparative estimates are made after the work breakdown structure and task lists have been assembled, checked and coded.

- *Feasibility estimates*. A feasibility estimate requires some preliminary design to be done and is a mix of comparative estimating and fixed price quotations obtained for the major subcontracts, including quotes for expensive equipment, mechanical services and other building management systems. Construction project proposals are often based on such estimates.

- *Definitive estimates*. A definitive estimate is the most accurate form of estimate, and it can only be made when the project is nearing completion. By that time, all design will be long finished and many of the site costs will have been incurred. Only a small percentage of the project remains to be finished, so that only a correspondingly small part of the project's total costs remains in any doubt.

Cost estimates and the work breakdown structure

The work breakdown structure (WBS), introduced in Chapter 5, should be the starting point for estimating the direct costs of all substantial projects. The detailed list of project tasks can be developed from it. Later, when design gets under way, design drawings and specifications will be needed for materials take-offs to allow estimating in finer detail.

When the work breakdown structure has been compiled like a family tree, every part should have a code, as already described in Chapter 5. The same codes can be used as the basis for drawing numbers, cost collection, budgets and so on in order to establish a logical cost breakdown structure (CBS) that corresponds closely with the WBS.

Setting cost budgets

Basic departmental budgets

By doing some calculations, for which a computer database management program is essential, we can rearrange the cost estimates from the coded WBS and redistribute the amounts to the various departmental managers who will be working on the project. Coding is essential if we are to produce cost budgets for all departments working on a project, so, in addition to the work breakdown codes, we need to give each department a code. Each departmental budget will break down into labour, expenses and purchases (materials and subcontracts).

Treatment of below-the-line estimates

All below-the-line items are allowances that must be considered as sums held in reserve. They should not be part of the original departmental budgets, but should be held in a separate account. Then, when unexpected but authorized events happen that must be paid for, the relevant budgets can be augmented by drawing down from the reserve budgets.

However, this process has to be conducted with care. If a department is overspent entirely through its own fault, then that has to remain in the cost records and reports as an overspend: it would not be reasonable to let the manager responsible off the hook by allocating additional budget from the budget reserves. Reports of overspending (or underspending) are called *variances*, and analysis of variances is part of the process by which performance can be examined with a view to improving performance (and cost estimating) in the future.

Budgets and project changes

The subject of project changes will be dealt with in Chapter 11, but we should be aware here that changes in project design or scope are likely to affect budgets. When the client has ordered changes, the client can be asked to pay for them. So each change will increase revenue and all the relevant budgets can be increased.

The costs of changes not authorized and paid for by the customer will not usually allow budgets to be increased because they cannot be charged out to the client and will not result in additional revenue. These changes simply increase costs and reduce or destroy profits.

The project manager's responsibilities in cost accounting

All cost accounting depends on accurate and timely collection of expenditures. The method of collection depends on the kinds of cost involved, but the project manager will be expected to cooperate with the accountants in the collection of direct costs.

Labour costs

The usual way of collecting labour costs is by recording the amount of time that each person spends each day or each week on each job number. These job numbers should relate to cost codes for the various projects being undertaken. Times are recorded either on job cards, clocking-in machines or, very commonly, on weekly timesheets. Weekly timesheets may be actual forms but much modern project management software allows for timesheet information to be keyed in directly by the various workers.

When the times have been collected each day or (more likely) each week, the accounts department will work out the costs of those hours. This is often done using standard costing, where a scale of standard rates, depending on the grade or trade of person, is applied rather than using individual wages or salaries.

All managers working within a project organization have a duty to see that timesheet information is checked for accuracy and returned to the accounts department promptly, so that project and company accounts are updated without undue delay.

Timesheets will probably be subject to independent audit from time to time, especially when the times recorded are used for billing clients directly in cost-reimbursable projects (projects that are not sold for a fixed price, but where the client pays according to time and materials spent on their work).

Costs of materials and equipment

There are several ways in which materials costs can be picked up and recorded. One way, common in manufacturing projects, is to record the costs of materials issued from stores as each job is loaded into the factory. That method is of little use in most construction projects, but, fortunately for the project manager, there are two better alternatives.

One way is to record the cost of all invoices for project goods and materials, either as they are received from suppliers and approved for payment or when the payment cheques are sent out. This method can also be used to record the costs of subcontracts.

The time to control materials and equipment costs is when they are committed, which means when the purchase orders or subcontracts are placed. Then avoid making any changes to the orders. Once purchasing costs have been committed, they can be reported but it's too late to control them.

From the project manager's point of view, however, the cost information collected this way comes too late to be of any use in cost control.

The earliest possible way of collecting the costs of purchased items is to record the values of the orders as they are placed. These orders might be placed months or even years before the goods are actually received and paid for. Recording the prices on these orders gives very early warning of expenditure to come – expenditure that has been committed by signing each subcontract or purchase order. So the project manager needs to collaborate here not so much with the accountant as with the purchasing department. Collecting costs in this way allows for reporting at the time when the costs are actually committed.

Cost reporting

Costs are reported at many levels throughout a project organization, but reports for which the project manager is responsible will go to senior management and, in some cases, even to the client. A typical cost report will list the costs of all items in the WBS, and the pages of such reports are often put together in the same way as the WBS itself. So we might have one top page detailing the cost performance for all the items or work packages from the first level of breakdown in the WBS. The bottom row on the top page will show project totals.

Supplementary pages, going into more detail on each item listed on the top page, often follow. The total report for a very large project could run to over 100 pages, but senior management would need to be shown only the top summary page.

A common system of project cost reporting using earned value analysis

Figure 9.2 shows one kind of report page that is often used in monthly project cost reports. This example embodies a popular (but not perfect) process called earned value analysis (EVA). We need consider only the top sheet, which is always the summary page for the whole project. If further pages are added to break down each item from the top sheet further into the WBS, the results from those pages are 'rolled up' into the page 1 totals.

The method for compiling this cost report form should become clear with the following explanation of the entries to be made in each column.

Project Cost Report

Project name:
Project number:
Client:

Report date:
Page   of   pages:
Report prepared by:

A Item	B Code	C The original budget	D Authorized budget changes	E Current budget C + D	F Actual costs to date (ACWP)	G Value of work done (BCWP)	H CPI G/F	J Estimated cost to complete (E − G)/H	K Estimated cost at completion F + J	L Forecast variation at completion E − K
Page totals										

Figure 9.2 A popular format for reporting costs periodically on a large project

Column A

The first column on the page gives the name of each item from the WBS, with the top page being reserved for all the items from the first level of the work breakdown.

Column B

Assuming that the WBS has been correctly and comprehensively coded, column B will show the cost code that has been allocated to each item.

Column C

Column C should give the original budget for each item. This should be the basic budget. Below-the-line allowances in the overall project budget are held in reserve. These reserve items can be included in the report by giving each a row to itself. For example, the contingency allowance and escalation allowance might be shown as items on the top page.

Column D

Some changes in the project will result in price changes, so that revenue from the client will change (usually upwards). When this happens, the amount of the budget change, after authorization, is entered in column D.

Some reports have an extra column reporting the amounts of budget changes that are being considered but have yet to be authorized.

Column E

Column E shows the current total budget for each item. This is the original budget plus (or very rarely minus) the budget changes authorized to date for the item in question.

Column F

Column F shows the actual item costs known at the report date. There might be some difficulty in getting up-to-date results from the project accountant in time, in which case the project manager might make some accruals. Accruals are what accountants call small adjusting amounts which are added to bring each figure to what he or she believes is the true cost at the report date (when the actual cost collection figures or cost claims are still in their various pipelines).

The earned value analysis process uses a standard set of abbreviations for the various quantities involved, and the abbreviation in the case of actual costs is ACWP.

ACWP is the actual cost of work performed at the report date.

Column G

Column G contains information that needs a little more explanation and is more difficult to come by. In earned value terms, this is the BCWP. What this means is the amount of work that has actually been finished, expressed in terms of what that work should have cost. In other words, it is an evaluation, in money terms, of the work actually done. This, in fact, is the *earned value* from which this process of analysis and reporting gets its name.

BCWP is the budget cost of work performed at the report date, which is the earned value.

For home office tasks, such as design, assessing the earned value of jobs in progress means making best estimates, so the figures are prone to considerable error of judgement if people report too optimistically on how their work is going. For work on site, the position is somewhat easier, because quantity surveyors can measure the amounts of work done and the results have a basis in real measurement.

Column H

Column H contains the CPI. This is the ratio of what work should have cost to what that work actually did cost. The result is found by dividing the earned value or BCWP (column G) by the actual cost of work performed or ACWP (column F).

CPI is the cost performance index, which should be 1.0 or above to be acceptable.

We should be looking for a CPI that is 1.0 or above. Anything less than 1.0 means that we are not getting as much value for our efforts as the project estimates and budgets forecast. A CPI of 0.8, for instance, would mean that we have only achieved 80 per cent of the value that was expected from the money actually spent. This could also be regarded as an efficiency factor or 80 per cent.

Column J

Different names can be used to describe the figures written in this column, including costs remaining to completion, estimated cost to complete, forecast costs remaining, and various permutations and combinations of these words. Just to be precise, and to avoid any misunderstanding, what is intended here is our latest estimate of the expenditure yet to come in the period remaining after this report date to the end of the project.

The assumption is made here that if, for example, our cost performance index has been (say) 0.8 up to the date of this report, then it will remain at 0.8 for the remainder of the project. So the originally estimated remaining cost must be factored up to allow for this poor performance. Naturally the estimate of costs remaining to completion would be factored down if the CPI happened to be greater than 1.0.

In arithmetic terms, the estimated cost remaining to completion is found by first taking the total current authorized budget, then subtracting the earned value assessed at the report date and dividing the result by the cost performance index.

Column K

Column K shows the estimate, at the date of this report, of what each item is now expected to cost in total at the end of the project. This, not surprisingly, is found by adding what has been spent to date, the ACWP in column F, to the estimated costs remaining from column J.

Column L

In column L we are attempting to compare the authorized budget for each item with our latest estimate of what that item will actually have cost when the project is finished.

Any difference between these two amounts will be reported here as a cost variance. In the example shown in Figure 9.2, if we expect to finish an item for less than the budget, we shall get a positive variance. So, here, positive variances indicate cost savings and are good news.

Some companies do this the other way round, and take the budget away from the final expected cost, so that negative variances indicate savings and minus signs are the good news. This can be confusing for a project manager who moves from one company to another, so we should always be clear what we mean by positive and negative variances.

The BCWS is the budgeted cost of the work scheduled to date.

SPI, the schedule performance index, is used far less often than the CPI.

Schedule performance index

If we care to divide the BCWP by the BCWS we get something called the SPI, a calculation for which no provision has been made in our particular example in Figure 9.2. SPI is the schedule performance index and, like the CPI, is a measure of efficiency that should ideally not be less than 1.0. If we look at the project plan and check out the number of days or weeks that should remain to the end of the project, dividing that planned amount by the SPI should give an updated version of the time remaining, based on actual performance on the project up to the report date.

The value of earned value calculations

The earned value process takes up an incredible amount of time and effort from many people engaged on the project. It is not easy to collect all that data and get it complete and accurate as at the report date. Using a computer might reduce the amount of work needed, but some very silly results will come out if some managers fail to get their reports in to the computer on time. In the worst case, lack of input data can mean the computer trying to divide by zero.

Results obtained from earned value analysis are only valid for the particular report date. Many things can happen to change the predictions between that report date and the end of the project. The most likely outcome is that the results will turn out to have been optimistic because people have not allowed for all the problems that arise at the end of a typical project, such as commissioning difficulties and dealing with snagging lists.

So the earned value process, although it has its strong advocates, must be viewed not so much with a pinch as with a large sack of salt. Nonetheless, senior managers like to see these reports, so perhaps we should make the effort and please them. When I was a young practising project manager I used to do just that, and sometimes I even let myself be fooled by the predictions that I produced and reported.

Cost control

Now that we understand something about the nature of costs in company, cost estimating and setting budgets, we can go back to look at all the items shown in Figure 9.1 and consider how project managers in a typical company can help keep costs within budgets.

Generally speaking, the project manager can help to control direct costs but not indirect costs. However, this is not always strictly true and we need to explain things in a little more detail. Take another look at Figure 9.1 (p. 127) and think about how the average project manager might be able to influence expenditure, for better or for worse, on the cost items listed in each box.

Indirect costs (overheads)

In general, the project manager can have little or no influence on the indirect costs because these depend on higher management decisions. It is the senior managers who decide how much should be spent on accommodation, head office clerical and administrative staff and, of course, their own salaries and perks.

Project managers will, however, be able to reduce some indirect costs by avoiding waste on heat and light, not spending unnecessary amounts on communications, not making too many demands for administrative staff, using vehicles economically and so on. Companies must always try to keep their overheads as low as possible because high overheads have to be paid for out of higher prices, and that reduces the company's competitive advantage.

Some construction contracts will allow expenses that would in many circumstances be considered as indirect to be collected and recovered from the client. We are not talking paper clips here, but slightly more expensive items such as telephone calls, special printing, travel and accommodation expenses and so on. When that is the case, the project manager must ensure that all expenses which *can* legitimately be charged to the client *are* charged. These costs might be small in themselves but they can add up to quite significant amounts of money.

Reducing Overheads

One London company headquarters reduced its annual overhead costs simply by installing a telephone call logging machine. This machine recorded the costs of outgoing calls from each extension in the company and logged the numbers dialled. It cut the total call charges in a stroke from over £100 000 to £50 000, of which £25 000 was recovered from clients. So, by preventing abuse and waste, and instituting correct call charging, £75 000 was shaved off each year's overheads. The cost of the call logger and its installation represented a tiny fraction of the costs saved.

Direct labour and subcontracted trades

The project manager cannot always be held responsible for the direct labour costs, because wages and salaries are often set by senior managers or determined by national industry wage awards. So, it is well argued, a project manager's control should be based on the budget expressed in man-hours rather than money.

The best, and really the only, way to control direct labour costs is to make sure that every job gets done on time. This means seeing that all tasks are regularly supervised, people are given leadership and encouragement, materials shortages are dealt with quickly and design queries are resolved on the spot or as soon as possible.

Direct purchases of materials and equipment

Efficient purchasing methods will ensure that competitive bids are received for all high-cost purchases. All custom-built equipment must be correctly described in engineering specifications that have been checked for correctness. If a purchase order or subcontract is signed for a purchase price or level of cost rates that is higher than planned, then the amount overspent will have to be paid for out of the project profit.

So, the time to control the costs of purchases is when the orders are signed, not afterwards.

Additional aspects of cost control

Cost control is not an isolated activity, but is something that depends on a whole collection of procedures, actions and a positive attitude. Many of these procedures have already been discussed in earlier chapters but two more must be mentioned here before closing this chapter.

The first of these related procedures is cash flow scheduling and management, which is discussed in Chapter 10. This is a procedure that, in effect, forecasts the contractor's cash in hand or debt at any time throughout the life of the project. It is not the same as cost estimating and is a subject that technical staff often do not understand.

The other procedure related closely to cost control is change management. Methods vary considerably between companies. Chapter 11 will be dedicated to this subject but, in the context of cost control, we can say here that it is essential to avoid project changes as far as possible, especially those changes for which we are entirely responsible and for which we cannot ask the client to pay.

Chapter **10**

Controlling Cash and Progress

Many professional people in project organizations, including engineers who eventually become the managers of projects, do not appreciate the difference between managing costs and managing cash. But every small family builder does, even if they get it wrong – in fact, especially if they get it wrong. So we should start this chapter with an example, just to explain the difference between costs and cash, and reassure you that this chapter is not a rerun of the previous chapter on cost control. After that, we shall probe deeper into the mysteries of cash planning and control and explain some ways in which project management can help to keep the cash position healthy.

The Dream

Please imagine that you have never been a self-employed business person yourself, and have always worked for others. Now you work for a large construction company which is going to make a bid to build a palace for an oil rich sheik, for which the price will be about £35 million. You know you could build it for only £20 million, if only you had the chance. You are tempted to offer to build that palace yourself for an asking price of only £30 million. Then, in two years' time the sheik could have his palace for £5 million less than he expected to pay and you would have £10 million in your bank and could think of retiring very early. This project is going to be carried out in a country where weather is never a problem and there is an abundance of good cheap labour. So, should you give up your day job now and start dreaming about large houses and luxury yachts?

Well, of course, there's always a catch. Your monthly salary is about £4000, but most of that is taken up with tax, general living and mortgage repayments. You look at your last bank statement and work out that your current balance is around £500. You have another £5000 in your building society plus other investments worth about £25 000. You can't count the value of your house, because you have only just arranged the mortgage and moved in. You have no credit card debt and, as yet, no children. So, if really pushed, you reckon you could raise about £30 000 from your current assets. Many people might consider that to be a fairly healthy position for a young person. But how could you start to build the royal palace, assuming that the sheik wants work on site to start next month? That spells the end of a beautiful dream. Even if you could assemble the organization in a few days, you would have no money with which to pay all of them, hire the plant, set up the site office, buy the first batch of materials and continue to keep your wife in the style to which she wants to become accustomed.

You could try approaching your bank manager for a loan, but you would soon find that, although your local listening bank might listen, as soon as they could resume straight faces and wipe the tears of helpless laughter from their eyes words such as 'security' and 'collateral' would feature prominently in the ensuing conversation.

So you are faced with a project that is, on paper, a sure-fire profitable investment but which you cannot hope to start through lack of cash and sponsors. The best you can hope for is that your employer will appoint you as project manager for the royal palace project. In that case, you might get some benefit from reading the remainder of this chapter.

'Annual income twenty pounds, annual expenditure nineteen nineteen six, result happiness. Annual income twenty pounds, annual expenditure twenty pounds ought and six, result misery.' (Mr Micawber, in David Copperfield, *by Charles Dickens).*

Shortage of cash can strike contractors at any time in a project, not just at the start. The aim must always be to ensure that you get payments in (which we call cash inflows) before you have to pay money out (the cash outflows). This is called cash flow management, and it is the important subject of the next part of this chapter.

Scheduling cash outflows

After the flight of fancy just described, we must come back down to earth with a heavy but painless thud and consider how any successful contractor manages cash flow. Cash flow management can be something between a balancing act and a juggling act, ensuring that cash outflows and cash inflows never clash to leave an overdraft at the bank that exceeds the agreed credit limit. So, the first action in getting to grips with cash flow management is to know how much the cash outflows will be and when they can be expected to happen. This is known in some circles as calculating a time-phased expenditure budget. People who take time out to do the earned value calculations described in Chapter 9 would call this calculating the BCWS throughout the project life cycle.

Like many things in project management, all that is needed to calculate the time-phased budget is common sense and a logical approach. The sequence of steps – many of which you should already have taken by now – is as follows:

1 Make a work breakdown structure (WBS) and code it.
2 Expand the WBS into a detailed task list.
3 Extend the WBS codes into the detailed task list.
4 Estimate the costs of all the tasks.
5 Using either a bar chart or a critical path network, plan the project timescale in detail.

6 Decide on your financial control periods. Should these be weeks, months or quarters?

7 produce a spreadsheet with every task's costs put in the boxes on the spreadsheet at the times when you expect that you will have to pay the bills.

8 add up all items in each period to find the total project weekly, monthly or quarterly payments expected.

9 add up the period totals across the bottom of the spreadsheet to get the cumulative totals for the whole project.

Figure 10.1 shows the bottom two rows from such a spreadsheet. Figure 10.2 shows how the cumulative figures can be plotted as a time-phased expenditure budget. The graph is useful for showing how the rate of expenditure is expected to rise and fall. Charts such as this will be appreciated by higher managers who like to be given pretty pictures in their reports. Graphs which show project costs against time are known as cost/time graphs. They are also often called S-curves, because of their characteristic shape. In practice, however, it is the spreadsheet that will be of more use to the financial controller of the project, because it can show far more detail and the figures do not have to be scaled off a graph.

All figures are £000s

	2006				2007				2008			
	1	2	3	4	1	2	3	4	1	2	3	4
This quarter	120	330	650	900	1200	900	450	200	210	40	—	—
Cumulative	120	450	1100	2000	3200	4100	4550	4750	4960	5000	5000	5000

Figure 10.1 *A project cash outflow tabulation*

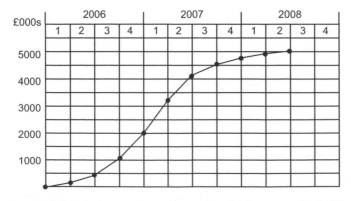

Figure 10.2 *A project cash outflow graph (time-phased budget)*

The time to schedule any cash outflow item is the time when you expect to have to write the cheque. This may be a little later than when the costs are committed because salaries are usually paid in arrears and suppliers will often give at least 30 days' credit before requiring payment for goods.

Scheduling cash inflows

The method for scheduling cash inflows is similar to that for scheduling outflows, except that we usually confine ourselves to spreadsheets and rarely, if ever, draw graphs. During this process we are forced to think about where the money will come from to pay for the project. The first and most obvious choice must be from the client.

We might also include bank loans or other advance financing as cash inflows, provided that the amounts and timing of these has been agreed with confidence. We could regard these amounts as inflows, even though we know that these loans must eventually be repaid, because they contribute to our authorized cash balance at the given times. Where loan repayments and interest charges fall within the project lifetime, these amounts will have to be included in the cash outflow schedule. If we do include loans in the schedule, we have to be careful not to mislead ourselves when looking at the total cumulative project figures, because an apparently large profit could include loan capital that has yet to be repaid. So it is really best to leave loans out of the schedule.

Most, if not all, construction contracts will provide for payment to the contractor in stages for the work done. The terms of payment vary from one contract to another, but can be classified broadly as either reimbursable or firm-price.

Reimbursable contracts

In reimbursable contracts, there is no fixed price as such, although there might be a maximum agreed limit. The client pays the contractor at the end of each month for the time and materials spent on the project. These payments may be at agreed rates plus an overall management fee, or they could be cost-plus, which means that the rates themselves include an element of mark-up for profit. This kind of contract is relatively rare these days because the client has to bear all the financial risk. However, they still have a place in internal contracts, where one company does work for another in the same group of companies, or for projects that cannot be properly defined and where the scope of work and difficulties do not allow the contractor to set a fixed price.

Cash flow problems in reimbursable projects should be low, because cash inflows should be received from the client at about the same time as the contractor is writing the cheques to pay the various suppliers and labour costs.

In the remainder of this chapter, it will be assumed that the project contract is of the firm-price variety.

Firm-price contracts

Firm-price contracts are agreed between the contractor and the client for a set price, based on a specified scope of work. The terms 'fixed-price contracts' and 'lump-sum contracts' are also used. Most contracts are of this type. The client knows the total cost to be paid, although this might be changed before the end of the works because of contract variations (see Chapter 11) and charges against below-the-line allowances.

There are several different standard forms of contract, each of which is promoted by one of the trade associations or professional institutions. These standard forms can apply not only to main contracts, but also to subcontracts. For example, the installation of an elevator will probably be subject to standard terms applying to the lift and hoist industry. Most of these standard forms will allow for stage payments, which means that the client agrees to pay the contractor for certified amounts of work done as the project progresses (usually monthly) or when project milestones are reached. A milestone is some easily recognized achievement in project progress, such as the initial contract signing, approval of final design drawings, the start of work on site or the time when the roof is made weatherproof and dry trades can start work.

Contractors' invoices to the client for progress payments are invariably accompanied by certificates from quantity surveyors or an independent engineer to certify that the amount of work being claimed for has been measured and is valid.

These interim cash inflows obviously help the contractor's cash position considerably and can mean the difference between commercial life and death for some contractors.

All amounts due have to be entered in a spreadsheet, at the times when their receipt is expected. Then we can work out the total expected cash inflow in each project period, and we can also sum up all these periodic totals to find the total expected project cash inflow (the expected revenue).

Scheduling net cash flow

So far, we have scheduled our expected project cash outflows and the inflows. Students often make the mistake of simply predicting what the difference will be between all the cash inflows and outflows at the end of the project. That process produces a forecast profit and loss statement for the project, but tells us nothing about cash flows and expected cash balances whilst the works are in progress. So we must compile a spreadsheet which includes both cash outflows and inflows for each accounting period, and which then compares the periodic and cumulative net totals. This gives a prediction of how the current cash balance will rise and fall during the life of the project.

LOX PROJECTS LTD | **Headquarters building for Megabux Investments plc** | Project number P21900
Issue date March, 2006

Quarterly periods – all figures £000s

Cost item	2006				2007				2008				2009				Total budget
	1	2	3	4	1	2	3	4	1	2	3	4	1	2	3	4	
INFLOWS																	
Initial claim		150															150
Stage claims			50	200	400	500	1400	2000	2750	2250	1500	1000	1000	1000			14050
Final claim															500		500
Total inflows		150	50	200	400	500	1400	2000	2750	2250	1500	1000	1000	1000	500		14700
OUTFLOWS																	
Engineering		40	160	160	40	20	20	20	20	20	20	20	10	10	5		565
Site preparation			10	50	100	40											200
Purchasing			10	50	150	350	800	1000	800	500	50	20	20				3750
Main structure					100	200	500	1000	1200	200	10						3210
Dry trades							60	200	800	1500	900	500	100				4060
Special systems											100	150	50				300
External works							20	30	20	30	40	40	40				220
Commissioning												20	40	5			65
Total outflows		40	180	260	390	610	1400	2250	2840	2250	1120	750	260	15	5		12 370
NET FLOWS																	
Periodic		110	(130)	(60)	10	(110)		(250)	(90)		380	250	740	985	495		
Cumulative		110	(20)	(80)	(70)	(180)	(180)	(430)	(520)	(520)	(140)	110	850	1835	2330		2330

Figure 10.3 *Net cash flow forecast*

Figure 10.3 is a fairly simple example of a net cash flow schedule for a project to build a large headquarters office on a greenfield site. The scope of work includes detailed design, initial site levelling and clearance, construction of the main building, installation of all internal plant and services, some special building management systems and external works and landscaping. The contract provides for the client to pay stage payments, the first of which amounts to approximately ten per cent of the total project price and is payable up front when the contract has been signed.

The inflows section of the spreadsheet has been compiled to show when claims for payment to the contractor are expected to be submitted to the client. The periods are quarterly because of lack of space on the page of this book, but monthly periods are more commonly used because invoicing tends to be monthly. Even if all goes to plan in this project, there might be some errors in the forecast cash flows arising from lags in submitting invoices and receiving payment.

The inflow scheduled for the second quarter of 2009 allows for a follow-up invoice to be submitted to the client in arrears for sundry works performed and not yet claimed, but the schedule assumes that all significant works on site will actually have been completed by the end of March 2009, which is the time scheduled for project handover.

There is a final payment of £500 000, to be withheld for six months after project handover. This is a retention sum, according to the terms of this particular contract, which safeguards the client to some extent in case there should be any dispute about the standard of the completed office building. In other words, the contractor has agreed that the client will only pay the full, final amount when all snags have been cleared up and the client is fully satisfied that the building conforms to the agreed specification.

The bottom section of the spreadsheet in Figure 10.3 is the section that will most interest the project accountant or financial controller. This shows the expected contribution of this project towards the contractor's total current cash at the bank. Note that there will be periods when the contractor will have to fund work in progress. This is quite normal, but the financial controller must ensure that funds can be made available from cash reserves or other sources to service the negative balance, which, it can be seen, will amount to £520 000 for several months at the peak activity time for this project.

The financial status of external organizations

The managing contractor is in the middle of at least two sets of financial risks connected with external organizations.

On the one hand there could be extreme difficulties should the client not be in a position to pay all the bills, leaving the contractor with a heap of work in progress, a cancelled project and a huge cash debt. The contractor will also be at risk, to a somewhat lesser degree, should any major subcontractor or supplier suffer financial failure during the course of the project, so that they are unable to complete the work ordered or repay the sunk costs.

The client's cash flow position

So far it has been assumed that the client will be in a position to pay within 30 days of the contractor submitting each certified claim for payment (some contracts are based on 21 days). Of course, clients can have their own cash flow difficulties, and it is in the best interests of the contractor to make certain that these do not prevent the timely receipt of any sum claimed. There are at least two things that the contractor can do to help avoid getting into debt through non-receipt of payments from the client. These are:

1 Investigate the client before entering into the contract to see if there is any history of debt, late payments or possible cash difficulties. In other words, will the client be willing and able to pay all the bills? Can the client afford to buy this project? Directly approaching the client on these questions would lead to a cooling of relations or resentment, but there are discreet ways of making enquiries. There are agencies that will undertake investigations on the contractor's behalf, such as Dunn and Bradstreet (visit <http://www.dnb.com>).

2 Contractors of large projects will often try to assist their clients in managing cash flows. It has been known for the contractors of large projects to help their clients to obtain loans from financial institutions. Cooperation can extend to providing help in submitting a case for getting a loan guaranteed by a guarantor (for example, the Export Credits Guarantee Department). Sometimes a project manager will work very closely with the client's financial officer by passing over and explaining the cash inflows section of the project cash flow schedule. Then the client will know the expected timing and amount of all future claims and should not be confronted suddenly by a huge unexpected bill for which funds have not been made available.

The financial status of suppliers and subcontractors

Purchasing agents and others who are responsible for placing purchase orders or letting subcontracts will need to be assured that work will not be cancelled owing to the financial failure of a major external supplier or subcontractor. Although it would usually be possible to find a replacement supplier or contractor, there could be punishing delays to the project and monies already paid out to the collapsed external company by the managing contractor would probably be lost and gone forever. The same process used for investigating the financial viability of the client can be used to research the status and past financial reputation of suppliers and subcontractors.

Fixed overheads add costs to the project without adding value.

Managing progress

In the previous chapter we noted that managing progress is a big part of managing costs. Any project that runs late usually costs more than its original estimates. There are a number of reasons for this, but high among these is the presence of fixed overhead costs, which will continue to accrue for as long as managers and other facilities are assigned to the project, even if no actual work is taking place.

Clearly, effective progress management will help ensure that claims for payment can be issued at the expected times, so that the contractor can pull in revenue at the forecast rate. So, progress management is an essential part not only of managing costs, but also of managing the contractor's cash flow.

The classic control cycle

Figure 10.4 shows the classic view of progress control. The theory is simple enough, and cannot be faulted. You must start with a 'work-to-do' list that comes from the project network diagram, after it has been time-analysed, resource-scheduled, filtered and sorted by the computer. Or, you might fancy working directly from a bar chart. The important thing is that you should be working to a plan. So, when each job is due to start, you issue instructions to the subcontractor or people involved.

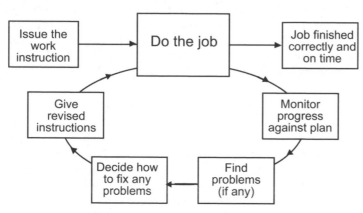

If you want to impress your friends, you can tell them that this is the cybernetic form of progress management.

Figure 10.4 *The classic progress control cycle*

Then you keep a firm eye on progress, and look out for problems. If a job seems to be running into trouble, take steps to try to overcome the problems and get the job back on track. All of this is good, basic common sense, and is the basis of progress management.

Don't take anything for granted but make certain that you or your representative keeps close track of progress. Snags can arise for many reasons, and we cannot list all of these here. However, here are some common problems:

- A job is running two days late, but otherwise everything is fine. Ask yourself: 'Is this job on the critical path or does it have plenty of total float?' If the job is not critical, accept the two days' lateness, but take steps to ensure that it gets no worse. If the job is critical, consider putting on a weekend shift or working later at nights until the job is brought back on track.

- A workman tells the boss that the drawings appear to be wrong. Perhaps the drawing shows a water pipe going through an area that is reserved for electrical trunking. Make sure that this is taken up with the design engineers at once, and that they are bludgeoned into putting the drawings right on the same day, if possible. You need to have a formal procedure set up for dealing with design queries, to make certain that everyone will respond quickly every time a problem like this crops up.

- Someone has ordered materials too late, or has forgotten to order materials at all, or has ordered the wrong materials, or has ordered too little, or the supplier has sent the wrong goods, or the goods have been lost or damaged in transit, or the supplier has lost the order, or they were delivered but someone nicked them from the site when your back was turned. Whatever the reason, if the goods are not available in the right quantity at the right time and in the right place, you have what is called in polite circles a materials shortage. When work is held up, costs go up and tempers rise too. So you must have an established procedure for dealing with materials shortages and getting the missing materials to site without delay. This might mean taking extreme steps, like hiring your own transport and driver to go and get them. Costs saved in not taking special steps are likely to be far outweighed by money overspent through the delay.

There are many problems over which the project manager has no direct control, such as industrial disputes and bad weather. Even here, though, sensible precautions can be taken to minimize delays.

It takes two to make a quarrel, and some highly publicized disputes in recent years have been caused directly by astonishingly thoughtless management actions or as a result of insensitive instructions and working rules. Of course, you will meet some militant and awkward individuals, but much industrial action can be prevented through consultation and by showing respect for people. Take safety seriously and maintain safety equipment properly. Listen to complaints and, if they are genuine, deal with them. Don't be taken by surprise. Have recognized procedures in place for dealing with industrial unrest.

Project managers can have plenty of power but are, as yet, unable to control the weather. Nevertheless they can arrange work so that as much exterior work as possible is done during fair spells and making the building watertight as soon as possible. Then when the bad weather comes, the interior work can continue. The schedule should make some allowance for bad weather delays, based on the season of the year and past regional weather statistics.

Managing progress in a larger organization

Figure 7.7 introduced the contract matrix, in which a managing contractor holds the project together, acts as the principal project manager and hires all the labour and subcontractors. For your convenience, a condensed version of Figure 7.7 is repeated here as Figure 10.5. Some subcontractors and equipment suppliers will have work so complex that they need to appoint their own project managers. Progress management of the larger project must be viewed in the context of this kind of organization.

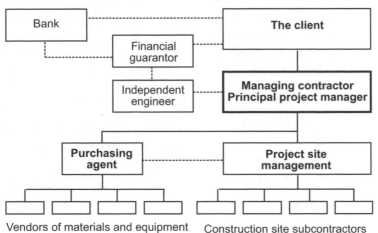

Figure 10.5 *Contract matrix organization (condensed from Figure 7.7)*

The project manager is at the hub of the project, and in the contract matrix is seen to be the principal point of contact between all parts of the organization. So the project manager not only has to plan the project, but must also communicate with all the key players in keeping the project on track and reporting progress and costs to the client. This means that the project manager must arrange the collection and coordination of information on progress and costs from all corners of the project organization.

The project manager will also be expected to provide any information and facilities that the independent engineer needs to certify to the bank, the guarantor and the client that claims for payment are truly representative of the work done at the end of each period.

The site manager

Clearly, the site manager has a very important role in supporting the project manager. Either the site manager or the project manager (or both) must try to make certain that subcontractors operate their own effective planning and control procedures. Some subcontractors have a nasty habit of diverting their resources to other projects when we need them badly on our own project, so the site manager will be on the lookout for areas of unusually low activity. Quality engineers attached to the site team will ensure that subcontractors perform in accordance with specifications and drawings.

The purchasing agent

In many projects that use a managing contractor the purchasing agent will be part of the contractor's home office organization. In other cases the purchasing agent will be another company, employed for its particular expertise or location. Partnership must be encouraged between the purchasing agent, the project design engineers and the site materials controller. All should work together to ensure that materials and equipment arrive at the site at the time and in the condition needed to fulfil the job. The purchasing agent will be expected to provide information on the progress of each long-term purchase order and might have to arrange inspection and expediting visits to some suppliers. So the purchasing agent will be expected to keep the project manager informed regularly on such matters as:

- current committed purchase order costs, including purchase order amendments
- progress reports on enquiries or invitations to tender issued
- progress reports on purchase orders issued but not yet supplied
- inspection and expediting reports
- provision of vendors' documentation, including installation, maintenance and operating instructions
- test certificates for equipment supplied, where appropriate
- any expected problems in obtaining goods
- progress on making good materials shortages.

Progress reports

Progress reports are often combined with cost reports and are issued under the project manager's signature monthly in versions for higher management within the managing contractor's organization and, of course, for the client.

Reports to the client

Reports prepared for the client should be concise, factual and well presented. In addition to a statement of progress, clients will probably appreciate summary bar charts and site photographs. Reports are often compiled with a statement of work achieved to date, a forecast of what is to be done in the next period and a list of any actions awaited from the client that are threatening or actually delaying progress.

Some clients require cost reports itemized by their own system of cost or capital appropriation codes. Such cost reports will typically provide a statement of certified claims made to date and the timing and amounts of claims expected to be made during the next few reporting periods.

Information provided to clients will naturally be edited carefully to remove any confidential proprietary data (particular on costs) but reports must never mislead. If internal problems are being experienced that can easily be overcome, these can be discussed in-house but need not be reported to the client. But any problem, technical or otherwise, that will definitely disrupt progress must be reported to the client as soon as its serious and irrevocable nature becomes clear.

There's no need to be too eager to cry 'stinking fish', but the client must never be deceived by false promises.

Internal reports

Internal reports for senior management are usually based on those prepared for the client, but can be more open in some respects, such as in criticizing internal failings or underperformance by suppliers and subcontractors. Earned value analysis reports are often included, probably using summary reports of the kind shown in Figure 9.2 (p. 134).

Updating schedules

Progress data collected must also be used by the project manager to update working schedules, to ensure that these take account of any damaging delays or, occasionally, progress that is ahead of schedule. Considerable detail is needed at this level of progress reporting, because each task that should have been completed recently or is in progress has to be examined.

Data collection can be by means of questionnaires sent out regularly from the project manager's office but this is now a rather outdated method, and managers and supervisors can be encouraged instead to key data directly into the project management system. The following are questions that each functional manager might be expected to answer, either daily or at longer intervals:

- tasks just started, giving the actual start date
- tasks just completed, giving the actual completion
- for tasks in progress, one of the following options:
  - how much of the task that has been completed, expressed as a percentage of the total task, or
  - the estimated duration remaining to completion, or
  - the expected completion date for the task.

When such data are entered in a computer system running modern project management software, an updated schedule is more or less automatically created. However, the project manager will also need to review the status of any proposed changes to the project (see Chapter 11). He or she must also keep an eye on the logic of the network diagram because, quite often, tasks are reported as started or even finished out of sequence, when the original network diagram indicates (obviously wrongly) that such work cannot have been done because preceding tasks have not yet been finished.

Meetings

People often complain that life includes too many meetings. One company has an office where the engineers always seem to be in their conference room, apparently leaving little time for any actual project work. There are many reasons (some might say excuses) for arranging meetings. But meetings bring people together to share important information, allow debate, resolve problems, review progress and make on-the-spot collective decisions. Listed below are the various kinds of meeting:

- project kick-off meeting
- technical discussions
- planning (including brainstorming)
- progress meetings
- emergency meetings to resolve disputes and problems
- meetings with subcontractors
- meetings with trade unions
- meetings with suppliers
- meetings with subcontractors
- meetings to consider changes
- meetings with the client
- site meetings
- topping out ceremony
- project handover meeting.

Some meetings cannot be avoided, but many can. Looking at the above long list, it's a wonder that we ever get as far as the last two. So there should be a meetings policy, ensuring that no meeting is ever arranged unless it has a useful purpose and will move the project forward.

There is good sense in combining some of the meetings in the above list, especially in projects with important subcontractors and suppliers, because those organizations should be integrated into the project team. Sometimes they can only be made to feel part of the team and communicate effectively if they all attend the same meetings. But, if there is to be argument and wrangling, it may be best to keep some meetings with the client separate. So, we can end this chapter by first considering a few principles about meetings management and then going into a little more detail on one or two of the more important kinds of meeting.

Meetings management

General arrangements

The person who is going to be in the chair at any meeting should make sure that the following arrangements are made, wherever conditions allow:

- a place for the meeting is decided and reserved for the announced day and time
- the current agenda, and minutes of any previous meeting, are issued well in advance
- the time and place will be convenient to all those asked to attend
- communications facilities are available nearby, but telephones in the room are either not allowed or are programmed for outgoing only calls
- the comfort and convenience of delegates travelling long distances has been considered
- refreshments are available when any meeting is expected to last more than an hour or so.

Running meetings

Some people argue, cynically, that meetings should be timed to start late in the afternoon, so that there is an incentive to get proceedings over and done with as quickly as possible. But people are more alert early in the day and are likely to have more creative and collective brainpower available to deal with any problems.

In project work, arguments sometimes arise because one party blames another for delays or other problems. The meeting is the place to sort these arguments out, and the chairperson should make sure that agreement is reached before the meeting ends. People should not leave a meeting feeling that that they were not listened to or that nothing useful was achieved. A strong chairperson will prevent arguments from becoming too personal, and will see to it that agreement is reached and recorded in the minutes before everyone departs. Actions assigned to any delegates during the meeting must be achievable, so that promises extracted can be honoured.

Minutes

The proceedings of any meeting held between representatives of different organizations with the intention of reviewing progress, making decisions or assigning responsibility for actions must be recorded during the meeting in a set of minutes. Minutes must be issued as soon as possible after each meeting so that they do not become outdated by further events before distribution. Minutes should be clearly and concisely written, combining brevity with clarity, accuracy and careful layout, highlighting each action demanded from any of those present. Every decision taken at the meeting must be recorded. No ambiguity must be allowed as to who is directly responsible for taking an agreed action and the date by which that action must be finished. Every person listed as taking an action must receive a copy of the minutes – an obvious point that is surprisingly sometimes overlooked.

Minutes must be accepted by all those at the meeting (or more usually at the next meeting in the series) as being a true and accurate record of what was said and agreed. It is important that the minutes are then securely filed or archived, because they may be needed as evidence to support a claim in the case of legal disputes long after the project has been finished.

Kick-off meeting

Many companies like to get their projects off to a good start by holding an internal kick-off meeting. The purpose is to bring together all the senior members of the project, tell them something about the client and the project, announce who is to be the project manager and generally give an outline of who will do what. The atmosphere is often informal at such meetings, and minutes might not be needed.

The ideal time for a kick-off meeting is just at the start of the project, as soon as the objectives and scope of the project are clear and authority has been given for detailed design work to begin. This is an occasion for a company director or other senior manager to give a gung-ho pep talk. The aim should be to send senior engineers, supervisors and managers away from the meeting fired with enthusiasm, ready to clear for action and start work, determined to do their bit towards building a successful project.

Progress meetings

Any project lasting most than a few weeks needs regular progress meetings to review what has been achieved to date, discuss the work that is scheduled next, and resolve any difficulties or problems. At the beginning of the project these progress meetings will probably be internal weekly affairs, held at the company's home offices to review progress on design and advance purchasing.

As soon as it is convenient, the emphasis on progress meetings will move away from the weekly internal home office meetings to monthly meetings at or very near the project site. Traditionally, site meetings are chaired by the architect or project manager, and are attended by representatives from the home office, subcontractors and the client. The site manager is a key executive and will often be the person responsible for taking the minutes. Site meetings usually end by providing the client's representative with a pair of wellies at one end, a hard hat on the other, and a conducted tour of the site.

A site manager for a very large London contractor used to get up from the table at the end of our meetings with the invitation 'Let's go and give it a couple of coats of looksee'.

Chapter 11

Controlling Changes

All projects are disrupted by changes. Even if there are no design mistakes (and that's an enormous 'if'), most clients change their minds to a greater or lesser extent during the works. Some contractors regard changes as a great nuisance, and one writer even described them as 'the cancer of contracting'. I take a slightly more tolerant view. Some contractors actually welcome changes requested by their clients because they expect work on changes to be more profitable than work against the original project contract. What is certain, whatever our opinion of changes, is that there must be a procedure for dealing with them. Otherwise our projects could descend into chaos. Most of the procedures described here are for larger construction projects and petrochemical and mining installations, but the principles of trying to avoid internal changes on the one hand, and dealing effectively with change requests from the client on the other, apply to every project, however small.

The writer who described changes thus was Peter Marsh. See the note below alongside Table 11.1.

Types of change

Changes happen for many reasons. Like risk events, changes that occur near the end of the project are likely to be particularly disruptive and expensive because they can lead to costly purchase order amendments and cancellations, disgruntled subcontractors and even the demolition and rebuilding of work that we thought we had finished. At best, work on site might be held up while fresh drawings are being prepared. Conversely, changes near the start of the project, unless they affect the contracted project specification and scope of work, will probably cost only time in the design office. These early changes usually fall into the first of the five categories identified in the following list:

1   Changes that are not really changes at all. These are chiefly changes to correct early design mistakes in drawings or specifications found during checking or by the designers themselves before these documents have been released for purchasing or construction. These corrections might cause designers some distress and gnashing of teeth and can delay the project but they are contained within the design office, have to be done, and need no further discussion here. If there are design errors, this is the best time to find and correct them.

2   Changes suggested by designers, the buyer or site management after drawings and specifications have been released for construction simply because each change seems desirable and improves the project in some way. If such a change really would save time and money and cause no scrap or rework it might be allowed, but every change request must be looked upon with a degree of scepticism. No change in this category should be approved unless we are certain of the benefits claimed for it. Of course, suggestions for innovations and improvements must always be encouraged, but extra time and hidden costs are involved in most changes. The client would be

very unlikely to pay for changes made purely at the instigation of the contractor or agree to any resulting extension to the project timescale.

3   Changes made by designers or requested by the buyer or senior site staff because of design errors or other difficulties discovered during construction. These have to be implemented, and will almost certainly be entirely at the contractor's expense.

4   Changes to the scope or design of the project requested by the client and agreed in a formal contract variation document. These changes are more fundamental and affect the project specification and scope. They will usually provide a basis for negotiating changes to the agreed contract price and project completion date.

5   Very small changes or additions or to the works requested by the client that can be authorized on daywork sheets.

General change administration procedures

The contractor should have a sound internal procedure for the consideration and approval (or rejection) of all changes. The procedure can be simple but must satisfy the following conditions:

Changes not chargeable to the client must be paid for out of the intended project profits, so such changes should only be approved if they are essential to successful completion of the project.

- Each change not funded by the client must be subjected to scrutiny by senior design and commercial staff to be certain that the change will not adversely affect reliability, safety and performance. The contractor should nominate senior engineers or managers who are to be consulted when each change is requested. These nominated people will be the authorized signatories, having the authority to approve or reject changes. They are sometimes referred to collectively as the change committee or change board. The number of such people should be small, but each person should have a nominated deputy so that a quorum is always available at short notice to deal with emergency changes. Three people will usually be enough, comprising a senior design manager, a construction manager and, possibly, a commercial manager.

- Requests for internal, unfunded changes should be made on standard forms which, in addition to a concise description of the change, must give the reasons for the suggested change, estimated costs and project delays, parts of the project that would be affected and so on. All people in the organization should be allowed to submit such requests because that will encourage suggestions, and no request carries any risk to budgets or schedules until the authorized signatories have approved it.

- There should be a cut-off point for non-essential change suggestions. Many companies operate a 'design freeze' or declare a time in the project when 'stable design' has been reached. This means that the project is about to go to the purchasing and construction stage and that henceforth only essential changes will be allowed.

The client should be given advance notice of the design freeze date in the hope that this will bring forward any contemplated requests for a contract variation and discourage subsequent requests.

- If a change is rejected, the person who requested the change must be told and given the reason why the change was not allowed. Sometimes that person might be encouraged to give more details or resubmit the change request in a modified, more acceptable form, so that it can be reconsidered.

- All changes requested by the client must be authorized on formal documents, either on contract variation forms or (for minor on-the-spot changes) daywork sheets.

- Approved changes, excepting dayworks, will affect the project schedule and the relevant drawings and specifications. All of these must be updated so that the schedule remains valid and the drawings and specifications record the true as-built state of the project.

Contract variations

Contract variations are a particular kind of project change. Their distinction is that they are requested by and agreed with the client, who will therefore be expected to agree to a price change and a revised project completion date.

One version of a contract variation document is shown in Figure 11.1. This starts its life by recording details of the proposed variation and, most importantly, giving the building areas, drawings and specifications that would be affected. When the contractor and client have negotiated and agreed the price and revised delivery, both sign the document which then forms an addendum to the original contract.

A contract variation agreed between the main contractor and the client can result in a number of variations further down the line in the organization, because the main contractor will have to ensure that all participating suppliers and subcontractors are brought into line with the revised requirements. Many, if not all, of these suppliers and subcontractors will have to be contacted before the variation costs can be estimated, so it can take some time to respond to the client and negotiate contract price and delivery changes. Table 11.1 sets out some of the factors that might have to be considered.

Lox Projects Ltd	CV number:
Contract variation	Project number:
	Issue date:

Client:

Project name:

Description, including drawings and specifications affected:

Prepared by: Date:

Effect on project completion date:

      Current schedule:

      After this variation:

Effect on price: Cost estimate reference number:

      Current price including variations authorized:

      Price change for this variation:

      Revised total project price:

Authorized for the client:	Authorized for Lox Projects Ltd:
Signed:	Signed:
Date:	Datè:

Figure 11.1 *A contract variation order*

Items for cost additions	Corresponding deductions
1 Design work for new or revised drawings, specifications and calculations, including consequential changes required to other parts of the plant and buildings.	Allowance for design work no longer required as a result of the variation order.
2 Site works directly related to the change.	Allowance for unstarted site works no longer required.
3 Site works required to other areas as a consequential effect of the change.	
4 Purchase of additional materials and equipment.	Savings on bought-out items no longer required.
5 Modifications to bought-out equipment on order or already on site.	
6 Costs of scrapped work in progress or goods received, provided these have not already been charged in stage claims to the client.	
7 Payments claimed by suppliers of goods and equipment for cancelled purchase orders.	
8 Cancellation charges from subcontractors for scrapped work in progress.	
9 Appropriate percentage uplift to recover overheads and provide profit.	A percentage of the above costs to reduce charges for overheads and profit.

This table is based on an idea from Peter Marsh's very practical book Contracting for Engineering and Construction Projects, *the fifth edition of which was published by Gower in 2001.*

Table 11.1 *Principal balancing cost factors of a contract variation*

Once a project variation has been agreed with the client, it can be treated internally the same way as any other project change, with the important exception that authorized budgets, target delivery dates, data for cost reports and the project price can all be revised to the contractor's advantage.

Daywork sheets

Daywork sheets can be regarded as very simple contract variations, but they lie outside the formal contract variations procedure and are relatively informal. They are used to authorize and implement work on small jobs that are extra to the original contract but will not affect the design or mainstream works. They usually have immediate effect.

Daywork sheets are often born when the client visits the site and makes on-the-spot requests to members of the contractor's staff. They are particularly prevalent when the contractor is carrying out works at premises already occupied by the client, so that the client is always on hand and has the opportunity to think up many additional small tasks or even try to grab workmen to do other unrelated jobs. Dayworks can sometimes get out of hand, as some of the following examples show. All of these related to one original contract for external extensions and internal improvements to a large suite of offices in central London.

The Perils of Dayworks

- The client noticed that new paintwork on an extension to the existing buildings showed up the poor condition of paintwork on the old building. So the client asked if, while painters were already on site, they might not just spend a little more time and move on to the old external doors and windows. 'Sure', said the contractor, who produced daywork sheets for the client to sign at appropriate intervals.

- The client asked for the big car park gates to be moved and repainted. The building works had changed the car park boundary. The heavy steel posts were embedded in concrete.

- The client asked to be allowed to dump rubbish in the contractor's rubbish skips, with the result that the contractor incurred additional skip hire costs for many months while the client continued to dump huge amounts of rubbish and unwanted materials that had been accumulated in large basement stores over many years.

- A site hut, intended to be in position for six months, had to remain on site for a further six months because of continued daywork requests from the client. So a rental rate for the site hut was agreed and recorded on daywork sheets.

- The client needed a 30-metre cut and cover trench for three 75mm cable pipes between two buildings on opposite sides of the car park. That was requested as an addition to the main contract, to be charged as dayworks. The car park surface concrete proved to be particularly hard and over 300mm in depth. Diamond drilling was needed to penetrate the massive main building walls and the angle of entry required three holes each over one metre in length. At one stage the drillers wondered if they would ever break through. All of this was charged back to the client on daywork claims.

Daywork sheets usually fall outside any change consideration procedures and are used alongside the more formal change approval system. However, each daywork sheet must be agreed and signed jointly by on-site authorized representatives of the client and the contractor. The recorded times are typically invoiced to the client at rates which include allowances for overhead recovery and profit. Daywork sheets can conveniently be printed as serially numbered tear-off sheets on duplicate pads.

Clients need to be aware that, although the informality of daywork sheets makes them a quick and convenient way of requesting what are, in effect, mini contract variations, the total amounts embodied in dayworks can (as the above examples show) quickly mount up to become a significant proportion of the originally agreed contract price.

Both contractor and client must retain their daywork sheets copies, so that the contractor can invoice all relating valid costs at the end of each month and the client can check that the claims are valid.

Changes and contract administration

When a contract variation or any other significant change is under consideration, it is prudent to consider whether any work that might be affected should be put on hold, in case it has to be scrapped later and replaced. That kind of decision is not for the faint-hearted and needs good judgement on the part of the project manager, because if the change is subsequently not authorized, some explanation will be expected of why the project has been delayed.

All authorized internal changes and contract variations affect schedules, drawings and specifications, cost control data and earned value calculations. Contract variations that bring in extra revenue will affect authorized budgets. Daywork sheets and contract variations will affect the amounts of claims certified for payment. All these activities fall within the general area of contract administration and it is important that all transactions, internal and external, are diligently recorded and progressed.

The contractor should appoint a clerk or other person in the home office to administer all changes, contract variations and daywork sheets. This need not be a full-time job, but it is essential that every change document is registered, serial-numbered and followed through all its stages to implementation or rejection.

The role of a project services or project support office in contract and change administration

The nitty-gritty aspects of contract administration are sometimes carried out by technical clerks working within a project support office. Such offices typically also include the planning and cost control engineers, progress clerks and, possibly, the cost estimators. Project support offices are usually led by a project services manager, who provides a valuable support service to the project manager of a team or to all the project managers in a matrix organization. To end this chapter, Table 11.2 summarizes the change procedures that will typically be monitored and progressed by a project support office or contracts administration clerk.

Item	Internal change	Contract variation	Daywork sheet
Needs documenting?	No	Yes	Yes
Serial number the documents?	Yes	Yes	Yes
Register the documents?	Yes	Yes	Optional
Keep the documents safe?	Yes	Yes	Yes
Will the main contract be affected?	No	Yes	No
Are time/cost estimates needed?	Yes	Yes	No
Change committee involved?	Yes	Possibly	No
Is our authorization needed?	Yes	Yes	Yes
Is client authorization needed?	No	Yes	Yes
Welcome as extra work?	No	Yes	Yes
Possibility of non-approval?	High	Low	Negligible
Will the client pay for this change?	No	Yes	Yes
Is timescale extension allowable?	Unlikely	Possibly	No
Will drawings need amendment?	Yes	Yes	No
Update drawing schedule?	Yes	Yes	No
Increase authorized budgets?	No	Yes	No
Revise cash outflow (BCWS)?	No	Yes	No
Revise net cash flow schedule?	Optional	Optional	No
Revise amount of costs remaining?	Yes	Yes	No
Revise total cost at completion?	Yes	Yes	No
Effect on overall profit expected?	Decrease	Increase	Increase

Table 11.2 *Internal changes, contract variations and dayworks compared*

Chapter **12**

Handover and Close-out

What happens at the end of a project will depend on many things, not least on the size and kind of the project. For some very small projects, such as those for private clients for small works, you can simply shake the client's hand and walk away, congratulate yourself on a job well done, and then go straight on to the next job. At the other extreme is the brand new office block with hi-tech building management systems or, bigger still, huge factories and petrochemical plants, where commissioning goes on for many months and where you have a continuing post-project obligation to the client to assist with breakdown and maintenance support for some of the installed plant and equipment.

The larger and more complex the project, the more involved is the close-down process. Closure activities can be costly, often using the time of people that the contractor would like to move on to the next project. For large projects, the contractor might even open a new mini-project, complete with its owns plans and budgets, just to make sure that everything is properly put to bed or laid to rest.

Closure activities, except for the celebration party, are unpopular with the contractor and all project employees because, unlike main project work, they are not creative and they cannot usually be charged to the client. Generally speaking, they add cost but not apparent value. Nevertheless, an orderly shutdown is necessary so that:

- lessons learned from the project are remembered and used for the benefit of future projects
- archives are assembled that can provide supporting evidence in the event of disputes and future legal claims
- the as-built condition of the project is accurately recorded
- effective post-project services are provided for the client.

Lessons learned

Everyone learns from a project, no matter how big or small. That is inevitable, because every project is different, with its own special risks, new design, new site and so on. Experiences from one project can strengthen our performance on future projects, even though those projects may be dissimilar in many ways. When a project comes to an end it is important to reflect on all the events and experiences – mistakes as well as successes – so that work on the next and future projects will have an improved experience base. The following are among the aspects that can be singled out for evaluation:

1 checklist development
2 project diary
3 retained design elements
4 retained planning elements

5   performance of subcontractors and the vendors of bought-out goods
6   site experiences, for improving work processes and health and safety
7   performance of the contractor's staff and the home office organization.

Some of these topics are discussed in more detail in the following sections.

Checklist development

Checklists are invaluable in many project management activities, and the experience gained from one project gives an opportunity either to compile or improve checklists for use on future projects. Here are a few applications where checklists can be helpful:

- initial definition of the project and its scope
- preparation of tenders and proposals
- contract terms and conditions
- initial site visits to investigate conditions
- quality issues
- health and safety issues
- content and format of reports
- meeting agendas
- security issues
- site preparation and organization
- risk identification and classification
- start-up activities
- project closure activities.

However, although checklists can be very valuable in saving time and mistakes, too much enthusiasm in their design can result in checklists that are far too long and detailed. Try to keep them short and to the point. The best checklists are those that are easy to use at a glance, perhaps needing just a tick in a box as each question is checked off and answered.

Project diary

Some companies allow themselves the apparent luxury of a project manager's diary. Here, the project manager is encouraged to retire into a quiet corner and take a day or two off for reflection, recording all the significant project events as they actually happened. But a project diary is not really such a luxury because it records information while the project and its events are still relatively clear and fresh in the project manager's mind. This diary does not have to be a work of supreme literary merit, but it should list dates of important meetings, any special difficulties encountered, either technically or commercially, and the reasons for taking the more important project decisions.

For most projects the diary will simply be filed and forgotten but, given the first hint of any legal dispute with a subcontractor, a supplier or the client, you can be sure that the diary will be one of the first documents to be brought back into the light, dusted off and eagerly consulted for clues or evidence. Project diaries should be written with this possibility in mind.

Photographic records can be kept with the diary. More usually, however, the most successful site photographs will be enthusiastically snapped up by the marketing department for use in subsequent publicity.

Retained design elements

Thought should be given as to whether any designs used in the project are worth saving, in case they might be of any use to the designers of future projects. This practice has been particularly worthwhile for manufacturing projects, where it is sometimes called retained engineering, but is less valuable for construction projects because each new project is so dissimilar from the last and, rapid changes in technology can soon render past designs obsolete. Nevertheless, specifications, calculations and general layouts can sometimes feed ideas to the designers of new projects. If any records of past designs are to be kept, they must be indexed in such a way that they can easily be rediscovered when they are needed. This can be done using standard work breakdown codes or by keyword searches.

Reinventing the wheel is not always necessary and can introduce new mistakes.

Retained planning elements

Network diagrams and resource schedules for a new project are often developed after an initial meeting at which several fairly senior managers and engineers are present. These people are asked to use their imagination and best efforts to produce practical plans that can be executed with minimum cost and use the best working practices that can be devised. So every new plan embodies a considerable amount of combined experience, usually expressed in some kind of network diagram.

Although it is unlikely that a network diagram produced for one project could ever be used again on a different project, elements within a network that will repeat in new works can usually be found. These can be thought of as small network modules. They can even be stored in a computer as a library of such modules. Modules can occasionally be revised to take advantage of improved methods, to refine duration estimates or simply to correct mistakes. There are several advantages to be gained from storing planning elements in this way. Each element will:

- build on past experience
- be devoid of bugs, which will have already been discovered and eliminated in previous versions
- reduce the time needed at future planning meetings, with obvious cost savings
- allow new project schedules to be available for use more quickly than if they had been developed completely from scratch.

The ultimate goal when using modular networks (also known as templates) is for the computer to draw networks entirely from library modules. There is more on this subject in Chapter 14 of the eighth edition of my book, Project Management, published by Gower in 2003.

This is an interesting area for project planning specialists to investigate further, provided that their companies can make the time, costs and facilities available. For example, one company developed computer library files and macro-programs that generated all the materials ordering, listed detailed work tasks and automatically drew the relevant part of the network diagram every time a summary task such as 'prepare foundations' or 'plaster walls' was entered by the planner. Whilst not every company can hope to achieve this level of sophistication, project closure is a good opportunity to see what can be saved for use on future projects.

Performance of subcontractors and vendors

All purchasing managers and agents worthy of their titles and salaries will develop a fund of experience on the performance that can be expected from different suppliers, equipment manufacturers and subcontractors. All this intelligence forms part of a process that is often called vendor rating.

The end of a project is a convenient time to consider how well all the external companies engaged in the project performed. Did they deliver on time? Were the goods as specified in the purchase orders? How flexible were suppliers to purchase order amendments? Was there any evidence of financial weakness? Did they provide installation, operating and maintenance instructions in the required language, on time and in the specified quantities? The project manager and the purchasing organization should review their experiences so that a vendor rating file on each external company can be either initiated or updated.

Handover timing and snagging lists

Snagging lists are supposed to be one of the last things a contractor has to deal with before handing a project over to the client. The idea is that the client inspects the building, notes all the obvious defects and then gives the list of defects to the contractor, who attends to them all before the final handover and Grand Opening Day. That's the ideal and dictionary definition of a snagging list procedure. It is generally expected that only minor snags will not be discovered when the client occupies the new accommodation. But things don't always work out that way.

The Dangers of a Too-Early Handover

Somewhere in England a client had been waiting well beyond the promised date to move all its staff into a new, large and very impressive office building. Annoyed at the delay, and impatient to get the staff in, the client was allowed to move in a little too early. When I visited these offices during the first week of occupation I was impressed by the chaos outside the building: landscaping and paths had not been started, and staff were gingerly negotiating their way over the rough ground and mud. A worried-looking workman hurried past me carrying a large mastic gun in one hand and a bucketful of refills in the other, obviously heading for the roof.

Once inside, everything seemed serene and beautiful, except that some areas were cordoned off from staff and visitors because construction work was still in progress. My appointment was on the top (second) floor. The lifts were still busy with porters moving in office equipment and furniture, but they were efficient and a vacant car soon arrived. The floor buttons were numbered 1, 2 and 3, in a building that had a ground, mezzanine and top floor. Pushing button two delivered me to the mezzanine first floor and a disembodied voice from a loudspeaker correctly informed me that we had arrived at the first floor. To reach the top floor, lift button 3 was pressed, but the ethereal voice correctly announced arrival at the second floor.

At the second-floor reception desk a wet mop and large bucket rather spoiled the effect, and the new white walls were heavily water-stained. The automatic skylights had opened too early after a rainstorm, allowing torrents of roof water into the building. Snagging lists, written by the occupants, were taped to the outsides of their office doors. For the whole duration of our all-day meeting, in a room with no outside windows, the lights switched themselves on and off at random intervals because the movement detectors had not been finally set, so at one moment we were brilliantly lit and the next we were plunged into almost total darkness. There were also problems with ventilation, and the toilets had other malfunctions that we need not go into here.

All the problems described above were temporary and soon fixed. It is now a fine building and no doubt a joy to work in. But many of these snags should have been fixed before the staff moved in, not afterwards. Contractor's reputations can be made or lost by the way in which they deal with the final details at handover. The project was already well over one year late, probably caused in part by the client's contract variations. One more month before handing over would have made all the difference between delighting the client and causing inconvenience and resentment.

As-built condition

Project definition, although usually thought of as something that is done when the proposal is prepared at the start of the project, is a process that cannot really be called finished until all the project work has been done. Only then can the true definition be known because of all the changes that seem to be inevitable for any project as it progresses from start to finish. The importance of keeping as-built records depends to a large extent on the type of project, but most contractors will want to file at least one set of complete design records. These become essential if there is any hint of a forthcoming dispute or action for professional liability following an accident or any other failure of the project after handover. In mining projects, for example, as-built records can be relevant for as many years as viable deposits remain in the ground, because clients have a welcome habit of asking for plant or mine extensions.

Drawings register

The most important document in the context of as-built records is the drawings register, because this records all issues of every drawing ever issued on the project, ending with the final issues that are archived complete with all changes incorporated. The bare bones of a drawings register are shown in Figure 12.1.

Some companies call this document a drawings schedule, and some keep a separate register just for the purpose of allocating drawing serial numbers.

LOX PROJECTS LTD
Drawings register

Project title:
Department:
Drawing number prefixes:

Rev. number:
Issue date:
Sheet of sheets
Project number:
Project area:
Originator:

Drawing title	Serial number	Issues record					
		Rev.	Date	Rev.	Date	Rev.	Date

Figure 12.1 *Principal elements of a drawings register*

This is a very simple example, and most contractors will have their own more elaborate versions. A feature often considered important is a section on the register sheets showing who received copies of each drawing at each new revision. It is also convenient sometimes to list the serial numbers of project variations or internal engineering change orders that apply to each issue of every drawing, although these details can always be found by looking at the drawings themselves.

Drawings registers are most conveniently arranged in some logical arrangement of subsets, each of which is the responsibility of a particular design department. So there might be separate sets of civil engineering, structural, electrical, piping drawings and so on. For a very large project the drawings are usually further broken down into site or plant areas. The project work breakdown structure usually provides the basis, and work breakdown codes often prefix drawings serial numbers.

Design calculations

All design engineers should be expected to record their calculations on standard calculation record sheets that can be referenced and archived in retrievable form. This particularly applies to any calculations that could have subsequent safety, reliability or quality repercussions.

If, for example, a structural engineer were to scribble all the calculations for a steel structure on a scrap pad, the chances are that those calculations would be lost the next time the engineer cleared out his or her desk. So engineers should be asked to submit their calculations with their drawings when the designs are independently checked before release for construction. These calculations should be held in indexed archives in case structural or other problems arise after the project has been handed over.

Purchase schedules

Drawings are not the only documents needed to define the as-built condition of a project. The contractor must also consider items designed and built by external suppliers. Purchase schedules are therefore compiled that list every significant purchase, giving details of the supplier, as well as the purchase order number, associated specification numbers and all amendments of these documents. Of course, it is not necessary to list every small purchase of commonly available construction materials. A useful rule of thumb is that every purchased item that needs an engineering purchase specification should be listed in the schedule.

On a large project, purchase schedules may be set up in subsets that correspond to, and are filed with, the drawing register subsets.

Vendors' drawings and other documents

Whenever complex bought-out equipments are installed in projects, the client has a right to expect full sets of operating and maintenance instructions. The contractor will have a duty to order these from the relevant equipment vendors and pass them on to the client.

Some contractors, quite prudently, obtain and keep their own copies of such maintenance and operating instructions. The suppliers of bought-out equipment sometimes cease trading, are taken over by other companies, or might not keep adequate records.

Vendors are often asked to supply other documents, such as installation drawings, parts lists, consumable spares lists, test certificates and so on. Experienced contractors will keep copies of all these documents in archives for several years after the end of each project. These documents might be needed to support subsequent post-project services that the client expects from the contractor.

It is useful and usual to stamp filing reference numbers on all vendors' documents as soon as they are received. A common method is to prefix every document number by the original purchase order number. So if equipment was ordered on purchase order number ABC1234, the vendor's documents supplied along with that order would be registered, numbered and filed as ABC1234-001, ABC1234-002, ABC1234-003 and so on. Whenever it is necessary to retrieve a document from these archives, the search starts by looking at the project's purchase schedules to find the relevant purchase order number, and that will lead the searcher to the appropriate part of the register, and from there quickly to the individual documents.

Closure administration

When a project comes to an end there is often a tendency for staff to continue charging their time against the project, even though all work on the project has actually been finished. There must, therefore, be a formal method for closing a project, and for preventing people from booking their time to the old project number. There are two actions to be taken in this respect:

1 Inform all concerned that the project is officially closed to further time and cost bookings.
2 Program a filter into the computer so that it cannot accept timesheet bookings to the old project number.

For approved close-down activities, it is often a good idea to open a new project number with strictly limited budgets and program the computer so that it will accept bookings only from the few people who are assigned to carry out the close-down activities. The accounts department will, however, need to keep their books for the old project open for a further few months, to allow for late claims from suppliers and other sundry straggling costs.

Handover and close-out

Writing this book has been a small project in itself. Now the time has come to close it down and hand it over to you, the readers. I'm sorry it was not possible to invite you to a handover party, but let me at least practise what I have been preaching in this chapter. I shall close out with a combined 'project diary' and record of 'lessons learned'.

Project definition, scope and organization

This book is one of a series, so we should consider the series as the whole project. Writing this particular book was therefore a subproject of the whole series. The work breakdown structure in Figure 12.2 shows the scope of work and some of the individual tasks. This chart ignores production and printing, and is concerned only with producing the initial manuscripts. Level 1 is the whole project, with each book a subproject at level 2.

In construction project terms, we might think of the total project as a number of high-rise buildings, with each book being one of the buildings. Then, to continue the comparison, each building has a number of floors, corresponding to the chapters in these books.

The organization had several interested parties and was not unlike the contract matrix common in construction projects (illustrated in Figure 7.7 on p. 97). For this book project, you, the readers, are the end-users. If this had been a construction project you could be compared with the occupiers of the buildings. Gower Publishing was effectively the 'main contractor'. The Construction Industry Training Board could in some ways be regarded as 'the client'. Two external consulting editors acted as the 'professional independent engineers', providing expert advice and guidance to all the other parties.

The contract matrix for this book project is shown in Figure 12.3. Each author fits into the organization pattern like a 'subcontractor', with their individual contracts made with Gower as main contractor. The construction industry uses model forms of contract in many cases, and this book project was similar because publishers' contracts run to a fairly standard pattern. My own contract with Gower Publishing, in the same way as any construction contract, set out the obligations of each party and specified the terms and conditions, including a performance specification and a delivery deadline.

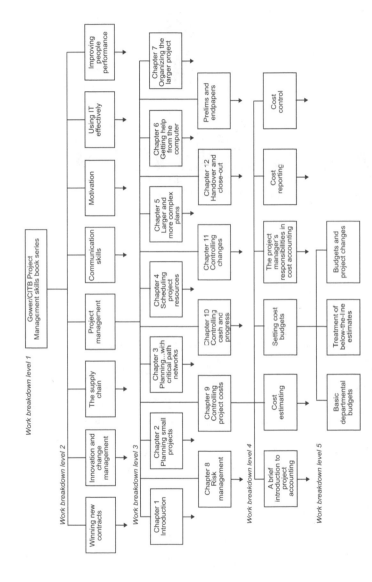

Figure 12.2 *Part of an early work breakdown structure for a book project*

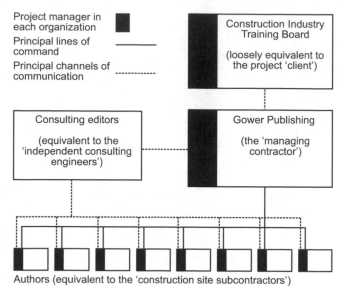

Project manager in each organization	■
Principal lines of command	─────
Principal channels of communication	┈┈┈┈

Construction Industry Training Board

(loosely equivalent to the project 'client')

Consulting editors

(equivalent to the 'independent consulting engineers')

Gower Publishing

(the 'managing contractor')

Authors (equivalent to the 'construction site subcontractors')

Figure 12.3 *The book project organization seen as a contract matrix*

Compare this 'contract matrix' with the construction contract matrix shown in Figure 7.7 and note the similarities.

Project planning

I could have used a critical path network to plan this project but you will find, as I did, that a simple bar chart is often adequate for very small projects.

The contract for this project became effective at the beginning of August 2003 and stipulated completion by 31 December, which allowed five months. However, other work delayed the start of this book until the beginning of September. I set myself a target of three months, aiming to deliver the manuscript one calendar month early. With 12 chapters to write, this meant writing at the rate of one chapter per week. In practice some chapters took a little longer than one week, whereas others were written in a few days. Although the plan (like most plans) was not entirely accurate, it gave me the control framework needed to ensure that this project finished on time. The bar chart is shown in Figure 12.4.

All project management is common sense. This includes choosing the right method to solve each management problem. We don't need critical path networks if all the jobs in our project run in a straight sequence, with one job following on the heels of another and no two jobs taking place at the same time.

A risk was taken in continuing to write Chapter 2 whilst the first chapter awaited comment and approval from the consulting editor. Fortunately this approval was received within a few days.

A computer is needed for larger projects, but the choice of hardware and software is down to common sense. Microsoft Project running on a laptop would have been fine for this project and is suitable for many projects. More expensive software would be needed for effective planning and resource management of very large projects or multiple projects. There is an abundant choice of software, but expert help may be needed with choosing because it is easy to waste money on a system that is either too small or too big.

There is no sense or need in spending a large proportion of your total project costs on a computer planning system. Choose carefully and buy the system best suited to your projects.

If time is short, we can often start some tasks without waiting for their preceding tasks to be completely finished and signed off. For example, we can order some materials before a building section has been designed. Overlapping tasks in this way speeds up the project but increases the risk of scrap and rework. The process is called 'fast-tracking'.

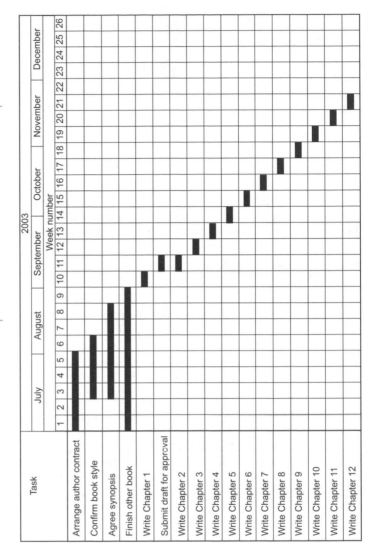

Figure 12.4 *Bar chart plan for preparing the manuscript for this book*

Cash flow and cost management

The execution costs for my subproject were low, comprising astonishingly large amounts of paper and printer supplies, photocopying, and other sundry home office costs. The contract included stage payment terms and, with other income sources, there was no cash flow problem. However, many small construction companies do suffer cash flow problems, and this aspect of project management must always be taken very seriously. Cash flow problems become worse if progress falls behind schedule, so that claims for payment cannot be issued on time. You also have to make sure that your clients pay you on time.

Risk management

One risk common to construction projects that was absent from my subproject was bad weather because writers do at least have the luxury of being able to work in their offices. There were only a few threats to the successful completion of this sub-project:

1   personal illness or breakdown
2   computer breakdown
3   loss of hard-copy manuscript in the mail.

Sensible steps were taken to minimize these risks, including back-up power supplies for the computer and daily back-ups to disk of all data. The manuscript was delivered to Gower Publishing by hand.

Project progressing and reporting

All project progressing should start with a kick-off meeting, and this project was no exception. All the parties shown in the contract matrix (Figure 12.3) were invited to a kick-off meeting in the London offices of the main contractor (Gower). This gave us all the opportunity of establishing communications and ensured that everyone started along the right lines towards successful project completion.

The end of each job on my bar chart was seen as a target that I had to meet or beat. When progress appeared to be falling behind, more time and resources were made available to get the project back on track (which in my case simply meant getting up at 5.00 am and working a bit harder). Both the 'main contractor' and the 'independent consulting engineer' were kept informed of progress by regular e-mails.

Effective progress management is only possible if there is a plan that sets out the time targets in clear detail.

Handover and snagging lists

This manuscript was finished in mid-November and taken to Gower Publishing in Aldershot on 26 November, approximately five weeks earlier than the contract date. There were no serious non-conformances with the specification. However, a detailed (and welcome) inspection by the consulting editor resulted in a 'snagging list', which revealed a number of minor mistakes and suggested an additional section. No contract variation was needed, and the additional section was completed and delivered to the main contractor on 6 January 2004.

Lessons learned

No matter how experienced we are, we all learn something new from each project that we manage because every project is different from all other projects. However, if you are entirely new to project management you should find that you can learn lessons outside the projects themselves. All of us who have project management skills use them in everyday life not just to manage commercial projects, but also to plan holidays, weddings and so on. Many companies that never carry out industrial projects nevertheless treat and manage internal organizational changes, office relocations, new computer installations as internal projects and use project management methods.

So, the biggest lesson of all is that many things that we do, both in our business and private lives, can be considered and managed as projects. If we define our projects accurately, then organize, plan and progress them effectively, we and all our project stakeholders should be well satisfied.

In recent years project management has attracted a number of good writers and there are several excellent texts available – many more in fact than are listed here. I have confined my choices to books at the lower end of the price range, but I have also included a few higher-priced books that cover related subjects, such as risk management and insurance.

Burke, Rory (1999), *Project Management: Planning and Control*, 3rd edn, Chichester: Wiley.

Chapman, C.B. and Ward, S.A. (1997), *Project Risk Management: Processes, Techniques and Insights*, Chichester: Wiley.

Chapman, C.B. and Ward, S.A. (2002), *Managing Project Risk and Uncertainty*, Chichester: Wiley.

Co-ordinating Committee for Project Information (1998), *Common Arrangement of Work Sections for Building Works*, London: Construction Project Information Committee. This guide, which is relevant to the compilation of work breakdown structures and cost estimates, is available from the RIBA Bookshop (http://www.ribabookshops.com).

Devaux, S.A. (1999), *Total Project Control: A Manager's Guide to Integrated Planning, Measuring and Tracking*, New York: Wiley.

Gray, F.G. and Larson, E.W. (2002), *Project Management: the Managerial Process*, 2nd edn, Singapore: McGraw-Hill.

Grey, S. (1995), *Practical Risk Assessments for Project Management*, Chichester: Wiley.

Institution of Civil Engineers and the Institute of Actuaries (1998), *Risk Analysis and Management for Projects*, London: Thomas Telford.

Lock, D. (2003), *Project Management,* 8th edn, Aldershot: Gower.

Loftus, J. (ed.) (1999), *Project Management of Multiple Projects and Contracts*, London: Thomas Telford.

Marsh, P.D.V. (2001), *Contracting for Engineering and Construction Projects*, 5th edn, Aldershot: Gower.

Reiss, G. (1995), *Project Management Demystified: Today's Tools and Techniques*, 2nd edn, London: Spon.

Reiss, G. (1996), *Programme Management Demystified: Managing Multiple Projects Successfully*, London: Spon.

Turner, R. (ed.), (2003), *Contracting for Project Management*, Aldershot: Gower.

Webb, A. (2003), *The Project Manager's Guide to Handling Risk*, Aldershot: Gower.